NEW PERSPECTIVES ON SECURITY

Also available from Brassey's

DANDO/ROGERS
A Violent Peace
Global Security After the Gulf War

GOW
Iraq, the Gulf Conflict and the World Community

ISRAELI
Muslim Fundamentalism in Israel

LONDON DEFENCE STUDIES
Published by Brassey's for the Centre for Defence Studies, King's College,
London

NAVIAS
Going Ballistic
The Build-up of Missiles in the Middle East

RODLEY
To Loose the Bands of Wickedness
International Intervention in Defence of Human Rights

BELLAMY
Expert Witness
A Defence Correspondent's Gulf War

CENTRE FOR DEFENCE STUDIES
Brassey's Defence Yearbook 1993

NEW PERSPECTIVES ON SECURITY

Edited by
MICHAEL CLARKE

The Centre for Defence Studies

BRASSEY'S (UK)

LONDON * NEW YORK

First English edition 1993

UK editorial offices: Brassey's, 165 Great Dover Street, London SE1 4YA
USA orders: Macmillan Publishing Company, Front and Brown Streets,
Riverside, NJ 08075
orders: Marston Book Services, PO Box 87, Oxford OX2 ODT

Distributed in North America to booksellers and wholesalers by the
Macmillan Publishing Company, NY, NY

Library of Congress Cataloging in Publication Data
available

British Library Cataloguing in Publication Data
A catalogue record for this book is
available from the British Library

ISBN 0 08 041790 6 case
ISBN 0 08 041789 2 paper

Printed in Great Britain by B.P.C.C. Wheatons Ltd., Exeter

Contents

Preface

The chapters in this book are the revised texts of the Brassey's Lectures on Security that were given at the Centre for Defence Studies in the early months of 1991. The only exception is the chapter by Wolf Mendl, which is the edited text of a lecture he delivered to the Department of War Studies, King's College, London, on the occasion of his retirement. It is included here because it fits well with the general theme of the volume and also in tribute to his distinguished academic career and as a mark of respect for the great contribution he has made over many years to the Department of War Studies.

On behalf of the Centre for Defence Studies I would like to express my thanks to all the contributors to this volume, both for their lectures and their subsequent revisions. I am also grateful to Brassey's for their sponsorship of this lecture series and for their support in the production of this volume. It serves as a good example of their interest in the Centre for Defence Studies and is indicative of their help and encouragement during the early period of the Centre's existence.

MICHAEL CLARKE

About the Authors

Michael Clarke is Executive Director of the Centre for Defence Studies at King's College, London.

Wolf Mendl was Reader in War Studies at King's College, London. He retired in 1991.

Barrie Paskins is Senior Lecturer in War Studies, King's College, London.

Brian Bond is Professor of Military History in the Department of War Studies, King's College, London.

Ron Smith is Professor of Applied Economics at Birkbeck College, University of London.

Philip Windsor is Reader in International Relations at the London School of Economics.

Christopher Dandeker is Senior Lecturer in the Department of War Studies, King's College, London.

Glen Plant is Director of the Centre for Environmental Law and Policy at the London School of Economics.

Michael Nicholson is Professor of International Relations and Director of the London Centre of International Relations, the University of Kent.

Lawrence Freedman is Professor of War Studies at King's College, London, and Honorary Director of the Centre for Defence Studies.

Introduction

Michael Clarke

The twentieth century is over. Indeed, in a political sense it has been over for some years. During the 1980s we began living through the politics of the first decade of the new century; this is one of the reasons why we found the events of the 1980s so surprising and difficult to understand. This assertion is more than simply an opening gambit in a political analyst's parlour game. It has important implications. As Barrie Paskins observes in this volume, the twentieth century was a short one; opening at around the time of the First World War, it was clearly over by the late 1980s.

During the First World War – in 1917 to be precise – the political processes that would shape the politics of the century began to operate. The year 1917 saw the emergence of antagonistic ideologies championed by the two powers that were to become the dominating superpowers of the twentieth century; it saw the beginnings of total war and the technologies of modern warfare that were to kill some 120 million people over more than 70 violent years; it saw the collapse of empires and the end of a pattern of dynastic politics, to be replaced by a growing number of secular, nationally self-determined states. Not least, it saw the beginning of an expansion of economic activity on a truly global scale that dwarfed the international capital movements and trade of the nineteenth century. Such developments shaped the political processes of the twentieth century on both the domestic and the international front.

By the 1980s it was clear that such processes were either passing into history or else were being overlaid by the more immediate and chaotic politics of a new era. The cold war was over, the world no longer so dominated by the superpowers, still less by relations between them. Perhaps there was only one superpower anyway. The world of independent states no longer seemed as coherent as it had during the previous 70 years, as new states of all shapes and sizes proliferated with the decline of the European empires; civil wars far outnumbered international wars; global economic processes had moved into a new gear and integrated international production began to supersede trade as the most significant global economic activity; a new age of religious international politics seemed about to dawn some 350 years after the world had assumed that secular politics had put religion in its political place; and new political challenges arising from environmental degradation, international travel and communication, and the internal challenges to previously settled societies, all began to move up the political agenda.

The political world we now face is, therefore, not merely new in the sense that it is full of things that have not happened before (for this is always the case), but our world is characterised by new political processes that appear to be stronger than many of the familiar political processes of the immediate past.

It is natural that we should want to take a fresh look at security after the cold war, for the end of that great antagonism must necessarily have an important bearing on our security in the future. But this volume begins from the premise that we would in any case need to look afresh at the assumptions we make about international security. One of the themes that is pursued in all these essays is the way security thinking and strategic studies throughout the twentieth century, and particularly since 1945, were determined by prevailing political circumstances. This is entirely understandable, though it has to be said that modern security thinking was also driven by prevailing misperceptions of contemporary political circumstances. Certainly the cold war – and particularly the elements of nuclear deterrence involved in it – was a major determinant of prevailing security paradigms. It dominated what was seen as important, what was ignored, what motives to conflict were assumed to exist, what constituted significant conflict, and even more what constituted a risk of conflict. But well before the cold war ended it was clear to most students of strategic studies that the dominant paradigms had become inadequate to explain satisfactorily either how security operated in the modern world or whence challenges to national and international security arose. For some, they explained security relations wrongly; for others it was merely that they did not explain enough. New approaches were required that could help us account, for instance, for the mainsprings of conflict in the Third World, the interaction of domestic with international pressures in defence policy-making, or the relationship between military force and economic magnetism as the bases for structures of security. A growing consensus among analysts that such issues had to be addressed in a different way and that bilateral and narrowly realist paradigms of security – particularly those that leant too heavily on theories of deterrence – had to be revised, predated the breach in the Berlin Wall in 1989.

What should these new approaches be based upon? A convincing, new, security paradigm is not readily available, though many radical approaches to certain aspects of security claim to be candidates for a dominant new paradigm. But the world of the twenty-first century is too contradictory to fit into a single conceptual framework. It is a world that is no longer essentially bilateral, wherein the pace of international political change tended to be glacial. Old-fashioned balance of power politics are in vogue again in an environment which changes swiftly and is becoming ever more 'multi-polar' as new states are born. But if balance of power politics – or 'concerts of power' – are again becoming relevant in world politics, then they share the stage with an unprecedented number of international organisations and a density of institutionalisation across the globe. Metternich and Bismarck did not have to contend with layer upon layer of international organisations through which their policy would have to pass, nor with multinational companies, instantaneous global financial markets, with mass media, nor with any of the other forces which have diversified and diluted sources of political power in the contemporary world.[1]

If we are to understand international security in the future we have to obtain a better intellectual grip on the nature of world politics in the twenty-first century. For international security is one of the defining characteristics of any international system: the existence of *insecurity* is one of the prime driving forces behind the desire of individuals to form collective units (such as states) in order to promote values and activities that make them feel more secure. If we understand the politics of security in a given era, therefore, we also understand the essential nature of the era: its politics, economics, social mores, and so on. Equally, we can only achieve such an understanding of security if we take due account of political, economic, social, demographic, moral and other factors. It is for this reason that we have assembled a group of essays to reflect interdisciplinary perspectives on security in general and strategic studies in particular. The task of explaining how our political world works, with all its contradictory trends, can only be attempted from a number of different disciplines.

This therefore represents not only an empirical, but also a methodological exercise. For in drawing together ten different social studies and humanities perspectives on security, we are also commenting on the study of security itself; assessing the relevance of strategic studies to contemporary world politics and examining the assumptions on which it is based. In one sense we are putting strategic studies in the intellectual stocks so that other disciplines – any one of which could fruitfully sit there with it – can, as it were, throw whatever they like at the subject. But such an unfair exercise is useful. Since knowledge develops in a dialectical way, all disciplines should do a regular stint in the intellectual stocks: those that do not rapidly suffer from what

Charles Manning once described as a 'hardening of the categories'. Moreover, strategic studies may be defined not as a discipline in itself, in the sense that politics, economics or law are separate disciplines, but rather as a subject that draws from different disciplines and which has enshrined some of the defining characteristics of them. If anything, strategic studies finds its place as a distinctive area within international politics, which itself is generally regarded as a sub-discipline of the more central discipline of politics. But strategic studies and the study of international security constitute a more important subject than this hierarchical arrangement implies, since it is based on assumptions about insecurity, units of identification, methods of settling disagreements, and so on, which are often intrinsic to the major disciplines within the social sciences and humanities. In sitting in the stocks, therefore, strategic studies carries important elements of other disciplines with it, and it has an ability to hold up a mirror to its tormentors.

This provides a starting point for Wolf Mendl's analysis, where he examines the confusion between the art of diplomacy and the practice of strategy as it has developed during the twentieth century. Strategic studies effectively began in the nineteenth but it was not until 1945 that 'strategy' was actively adopted as a device by the powers engaged in the cold war, not always with happy results. Now that the cold war is over, he argues, it is possible for the new international relations of the next century to go back to some of the basics of diplomacy and to rediscover the skill, and the political potency, of international compromise and accommodation. 'Strategy', in other words, should not be allowed to overcome diplomacy.

The philosopher echoes the diplomatic historian in the next chapter, where Barrie Paskins argues that, not only is the twentieth century over, but that its passing marks the end of a 'secular' age in world politics; a period of exactly 200 years, from 1789–1989. We now confront the need, he says, to rediscover some of the spiritual values that have been lacking, particularly in the violent twentieth century – the continued lack of which would threaten us with a world of capricious and meaningless violence and insecurity. Strategic studies have somehow to accommodate the fact that security is an objective human value (even if it is nevertheless elusive) and yet a value that cannot ultimately be satisfied within the natural world. The new age we are entering will be driven partly by a need to arrive at spiritual values that can be expressed in international politics; a development that could have profoundly positive or negative consequences, depending on the values in question and the way we choose to express them.

Brian Bond takes a historian's view of security and cautions against the natural tendency to try to draw historical parallels, particularly in matters of war and conflict. The tendency should be resisted, first, because a proper understanding of particular cases reveals more differences than similarities. The Munich crisis of 1938 did so much to create a popular image of 'appeasement', that there was a tendency to view Western policy in the Gulf crisis following the invasion of Kuwait in August 1990 as having 'learned the lessons of Munich'. But the situations will not bear too close a comparison, and the task of the historian is to establish the distinctiveness of each age rather than dwell on some of the similarities. Secondly, only in this way can we gain sufficient sympathy and understanding for the policy-makers of the past, thereby helping us appreciate the uniqueness of policy-making problems in the new age in which we now find ourselves.

Michael Clarke takes up the new age theme and examines the way in which 'security' has been handled both in theory and practice during the twentieth century. International politics has been distinguished from the study of politics – primarily the study of domestic politics – by the assumptions that both studies made about security. But this will not do in the new age. Sources of insecurity cannot be explained by reference only, or even predominantly, to the logic of international politics. The contribution that the study of domestic and comparative politics can make to an understanding of international security should not only be embraced, but regarded as mandatory by scholars in both subjects, however reluctant the domestic specialist has been to get involved in the international world. Nation states show no signs of diminishing in relevance in the twenty-first century, but the perceptual importance of their national borders certainly does. National boundaries have already become a deeply-flawed intellectual demarcation device.

From an international political perspective, Philip Windsor goes more deeply into why 'security' became the definitional heart of international politics. And if Clarke argues that domestic politics have got to adjust to a more internationalised world, Philip Windsor – while in no way diminishing the intrinsic importance of international politics – argues that his subject needs to think carefully about its values. It is still the case that wars occur because some states and some leaders actively want to pursue war – or may see it as a genuinely preferable policy option to their available alternatives. International politics still has to cope with that insecurity. But whereas security was at the heart of the origins of the study of international politics, Windsor argues that the situation is now reversed: international politics is at the heart of how we now currently define security. The subject therefore needs to conduct a dialogue of values to establish more precisely what it should be about and how it can serve the world of the next century.

Ron Smith considers the same problem from the perspective of an economist. Economists ask different questions about security, he says, and it could not, and should not, be otherwise. Policy-makers have little choice but to stick to certain frames of reference for long periods. But then major discontinuities in perceptions will produce political crises and a perceived need for quite new frames of reference. But the economist, he says, is more interested in longer-term trends and underlying conditions. In this respect the economist can lend to the new security perspectives we all seek an understanding of three major longer-term trends of great relevance to our thinking about security: namely, questions about the strength of the national economy and its relationship to defence spending; the decline of sovereignty as a politically authoritative concept; and the growing income inequality in the world. Certainly, he says, economic logic suggests conclusions for the security analyst that seem politically preposterous – until they happen.

The sociological perspective offered by Christopher Dandeker looks at much the same issue, but takes a somewhat different tone. He points to the way in which sociology has deliberately neglected the international world, mainly for reasons of methodology and ideology. But it is clear, he says, not that strategy has got to take sociology on board but rather vice versa. In particular, the relationship between the military and the state is fundamental to the way they are both defined. And that relationship is changing in a western society that is becoming 'warless' – not without conflict but predominently without official, state-to-state conflict. The extent of such change remains an open question, however.

Glen Plant offers the perspectives of an international lawyer on modern conflict. There have been celebrated cases in the past where legal advice was ignored by politicians in the midst of crisis, normally with counter-productive results. But he points out that it is in the nature of contemporary crisis and conflict that international law will loom larger. Despite the scepticism that is sometimes expressed about the efficacy of international law, it nevertheless remains law, and states would much rather be seen to abide by it than flout it. Legal advisers, of various sorts, are required by modern states and their subject covers a growing range of matters that have to be addressed during multinational crises in a highly complex world.

Michael Nicholson provides a conflict researcher's perspective on security. Conflict research, he argues, is not merely a subject area but a methodological approach to the study of human conflict. Whereas international security has grown out of history and other humanities subjects and is informed by a scepticism that human affairs can be analysed only by humanistic rather than scientific means, Michael Nicholson is clear that conflict analysis *is* the attempt to quantify and analyse systematically the various dimensions of conflict. From this perspective there is no reason to regard the state as the basic unit to which security matters should apply. Individuals are often made more insecure by their own governments and societies than by most of the events in the international world. Conflict analysis is interested in all types of conflict – personal, domestic and international – and it regards the security of individuals as the starting point and rationale of the study. For the future, we are confronted by a number of problems. In the short term aggressive and revisionist states are likely to persist and the prospects of international war are not likely to diminish. So we will need the strategist for some time yet and, in particular, to study stable distributions of power that can restrain such states. In the longer term, we need to know what makes states become authoritarian or expansionary, and in the longest term, we have to be prepared to confront the human reaction to violence. It is not sufficient, says Nicholson, to regard violence as a human aberration. We are appalled but also fascinated by it, and to pretend that human violence is simply that which is generated by political units (such as states) is to ignore a major part of the human psyche.

Finally, on behalf of strategic studies, Lawrence Freedman considers whether the acknowledged need to open the subject up to other disciplines is an exercise in mere eclecticism or a creative synthesis. The titles we use to describe different disciplines and the demarcation lines between them are not issues on which we should spend too much time or energy. Instead, he looks for the essential elements in strategic studies – elements that must borrow and draw from many other subjects. Strategy is the matter of relating ends to means: it is intrinsically connected to the exercise of political power. During the cold war, strategic studies viewed the exercise of power essentially as a function of the degree of stability in the relations between states. But stability became a fetish in the discipline and there is a general recognition now that the achievement of strategic stability in such a complex world not only must depend on a delicate balance of military and non-military measures, but the very pursuit of overt stability may be a chimera. Nevertheless, strategy remains concerned with the exercise of power. Power may be exercised at one end of the spectrum as authority; at the other as coercion and in both guises strategy can only understand power by drawing from other disciplines. There are many ways in which other subjects in the humanities and the social sciences should be integrated into the study of strategy; indeed it is in the nature of strategy that in studying conditions of relative instability and inherent conflict a unified theory is very unlikely to emerge. Strategy has to be eclectic. But if it encourages the study of disorder and instability, then it is merely reflecting some of the realities of world politics and it can claim a place of some importance for that alone.

As we face the new international world of the twenty-first century, therefore, we face a renewed need to try to strip away from strategic studies and the other disciplines and subdisciplines represented in this volume some of the ideological baggage they carried with them in a highly ideological century. In one sense, we are all strategists now; which is to say that security problems affect us all within, between and outside the framework of the state. If we seek to understand the workings of political power in our contemporary world, we will have to be prepared not only to draw from many subjects — accomplished academics have always done that — but to try to integrate the relevant insights into our own studies of security. We are unlikely to create a single theory out of this, since the variables will be too numerous and complex, but our own under-standing will almost certainly be enhanced. The world into which we are moving offers *prima-facie* evidence that nothing less than such an ambitious attempt at eclecticism will do.

1

Strategic Thinking in Diplomacy: A Legacy of the Cold War

Wolf Mendl

The dominance of military/strategic considerations in the conduct of international relations is the principal legacy of the cold war. It affected the two superpowers, their allies, and other major powers. The phenomenon cannot be attributed to bloc confrontation alone. There are many instances in modern history when such confrontations dominated international relations and military affairs played a leading role in the formulation of foreign policy, although usually for relatively short periods of time. Moreover, in spite of such preoccupations, the military instrument was usually seen as a means of last resort in the pursuit of national objectives, after diplomacy, the principal arm of foreign policy had failed.

The era of the cold war is unique because bloc confrontation lasted for nearly half a century and the alliances included integrated military structures in peacetime. Above all, it coincided with the emergence of nuclear weapons as the most important element in the military equation among the powers. The impact of those weapons has been decisive in confusing diplomacy with strategy.

The Impact of Nuclear Weapons

Although nuclear weapons have not been used in war since 1945, they have had a pervasive and revolutionary influence on relations among nations possessing them or depending on them for their security.

First of all, they require a state of instant readiness for war. They do not allow time for mobilisation or formal declarations of war, for a transition from peace to war. Hence the role of the nuclear strategist in peacetime is as important as the traditional role of the strategist during war. The nation must be on a permanent warfooting. The term 'cold war' is an eloquent expression of this state of affairs.

In spite of the constant attention to the possibility of a nuclear conflict and to the improvement of the weaponry with which to fight it, there is an awareness of the mutual danger in its use. Apart from a handful of academic strategists, no one seriously believes that there can be any 'winners' in a nuclear war. Hence the belief that the prime, if not the sole, purpose of nuclear armament is to deter an opponent. The concept of deterrence goes beyond the old idea, *si vis pacem, para bellum*. Before the nuclear age it was assumed that if deterrence failed, then war would be the natural corollary and could be winnable. In the light of the hazards today, deterrence must not be allowed to fail. 'Cold war' has therefore become a substitute for 'hot war', with the consequence that strategy (the instrument of military policy) has merged with diplomacy (the instrument of foreign policy). Contemporary literature, journalism and speeches are full of examples which illustrate the blurring of the distinction between the two. Take the former Soviet Foreign Minister Mr Shevardnadze, for instance. As head of the Soviet Union's diplomatic machine he thought it necessary to acquire the knowledge and skills of a strategist:

> It is an unending learning process. I am not alone. Many of us had to go through the academy mastering the intricacies of missile technology, of chemical weapons . . . Traditional bargaining has been left behind. Diplomacy has become more like a science, complex like calculus.[1]

In the nuclear age, the diplomat must have the knowledge (of missile technology or chemical weapons) that at other times was left to the military professional. He must also abandon the traditional skills associated with his craft (bargaining) and become 'scientific' in the sense that a strategist tries to be precise and calculating – activities in which the art of personal relations, an essential skill of the successful diplomat, is pushed into the background or abandoned altogether.

With such mental equipment, the diplomat becomes a strategist and his objectives are strategic. For example, when Acting Secretary of State Lawrence Eagleburger outlined American policy towards China before the Senate Foreign Relations Committee in February 1990, strategic considerations had priority:

> First, we have sought to nurture a strategic relationship with China aimed at drawing the Chinese out of their isolation and encouraging their co-operation on major international issues. While initially China was clearly perceived as a counterbalance to Soviet expansionism, its strategic role has evolved over the years to encompass a number of global issues.[2]

He went on to say that the strategic dimension continued to dominate at a time when '. . . we all recognise that the dramatic reforms occurring in eastern Europe and the Soviet Union have altered the strategic scene.'[3] and that:

. . . China's strategic significance needs to be seen not simply through the narrow prism of the Soviet factor but on the far broader scale of its place in an increasingly polycentric world.[4]

Regardless, therefore, of whether the original reasons for the primacy of strategic objectives in relations with China have ceased to be valid, the strategic concept continues to dominate even when the more traditional diplomatic objective of 'drawing the Chinese out of their isolation and encouraging their co-operation on major international issues' might be thought to have become the primary purpose of American policy.

The word 'strategy' has become synonymous with 'foreign policy', and is often used in contexts which bear no resemblance to its original meaning. Thus the Japanese Prime Minister titled his lecture to the International Institute for Strategic Studies after the London summit of 1984, as *Japan's Choice: a Strategy for World Peace and Prosperity.*[5]

One other important by-product of the nuclear dimension has been the penetration of the military/strategic domain by civilians. In the words of Paul Gordon Lauren:

> . . . to avert nuclear war and yet maintain security in the context of the cold war became a matter of vital concern to policy makers and scholars alike. The result has been an imposing body of theory created primarily by Americans and focusing primarily upon bargaining with threats of force.[6]

The concentration on 'bargaining with threats of force' has been furthered by the abstraction of war under the shadow of a nuclear holocaust. One manifestation of this has been the proliferation of 'think tanks', of which the RAND Corporation, originally set up by the United States Air Force, and the International Institute for Strategic Studies are the most outstanding examples.[7] By focusing on strategy, but in effect analysing the objectives and processes of international relations, these institutions and their publications have arrived at a 'self-congratulatory understanding that the science of strategy has come to master the laws of international relations.'[8]

As a consequence, professional military men, acutely aware of the messy realities of war, have been inclined to take a more cautious and realistic view of nuclear war and its effects than many civilian strategists. A good illustration of such a divergence occurred in the behaviour of military men and civilians when playing computerised war games:

> . . . the military is (*sic*) not the strongest advocate of force. It's usually the wishy-washy liberal or the political appointee who comes in and feels

very desperate and resorts to force. The ones who do frighten me are the scientists. God Almighty. Those nuclear boys, you know, the ones from the labs. They're deadly. They love to think in megatons this and kilowatts that.[9]

The combination of the impact of nuclear weapons and the confrontational character of East–West relations in the post-war era made foreign policy an adjunct of nuclear strategy: a trend that has been strongly reinforced by the practice of public diplomacy. The idea that one could '. . . apply to the conduct of *external* affairs, the ideas and practices in the conduct of *internal* affairs'[10], had its origins in Woodrow Wilson's slogan: 'open agreements openly arrived at'. Public diplomacy focuses on propaganda and the achievement of quick decisions rather than mutually acceptable agreements arrived at after long, difficult and confidential negotiations. Confrontation and conflict are the stuff of modern journalism and media bias towards that side of things has further strengthened the view of diplomacy as a form of warfare.

The impact of nuclear weapons, the cold war, and public diplomacy on our perceptions of the purpose and conduct of international relations must not, however, lead us to ignore the fact that the element of force and the threat of its use have always played a part in diplomacy. It is therefore necessary to examine more closely the extent to which strategy has abandoned its subordinate role in the conduct of foreign policy.

Foreign Policy, Diplomacy and Strategy

The spheres of policy and strategy overlap. Both are concerned with the achievement of specific ends, but there is a difference in scope between them. Policy may encompass strategy, whereas strategy has a more limited application. Foreign policy is '. . . the substance of a state's relations with other powers and agencies and the purposes it hopes to achieve by these relations . . .'[11] Strategy, on the other hand, is the 'art of distributing and applying military means to fulfil the ends of policy.'[12] In the final analysis, strategy, like diplomacy, is the servant of policy and only comes into full play when other means to pursue policy objectives are exhausted or become inappropriate. Clausewitz insisted that strategy should remain the instrument of policy during armed hostilities. However, under conditions of modern warfare, the aims of strategy – coercion and defeat of the enemy – tend to become synonymous with the 'substance' and 'purpose' of policy.

Today, the objectives of a nation's external policy are assumed to include national security, economic and social well-being, honour-ing international commitments, such as the terms of alliances, the protection of dependent territories and individual citizens, and the creation of a peaceful and just world order. Of these, national security usually heads the list.[13] Behind these assumptions lies the belief in the primacy of the national interest in a world dominated by the conflicts of competing nation-states. Nevertheless, there are various ways of dealing with international conflicts. Threats and the use of force are only two among several. Others include nego-tiations, bargaining, the search for and identification of shared interests, the development of economic and cultural relations and the strengthening of international institutions to deal with global problems and the management of disputes. All these approaches assume greater importance as economic, technological and environ-mental interdependence grows and international organisations proliferate.

The diplomat is the principal agent in the execution of foreign policy, for diplomacy is '. . . the process of dialogue and negotiations by which states in a system conduct their relations and pursue their purposes by means short of war . . .'[14] Idealists are inclined to describe the functions of the diplomat in moralistic and ethical terms. The fifteenth century Archbishop of Toulouse, Bernard de Rosier insisted that the business of an ambassador was to labour for the common good and never to stir up internal dissensions or war.[15] In the Nineteenth Century, Sir Robert Peel the younger described diplo-macy as 'the great engine used by civilised society for the purpose of maintaining peace.'[16]

Cynics, on the other hand, might think that:

> The first duty of an ambassador is exactly the same as that of any other servant of government: that is, to do, say, advise and think whatever may best serve the preservation and aggrandisement of his own state.[17]

François de Callières referred to the diplomat as 'an honourable spy'. The ambassador of James I in Venice went further and declared the diplomat to be 'an honest man sent to lie abroad for the good of his country'.[18]

Each of these positions contains an element of the truth. A diplo-mat's job is both to serve the interests of his country and to seek a peaceful and harmonious conclusion in the settlement of conflicting interests. His perception of his country's best interests may differ from, even clash with the perceptions of his political masters. The examples of Sir Robert Vansittart's opposition to the pre-war policy of appeasement and the *crise de conscience* of British diplomats over Suez in 1956 show that he is not always a passive, amoral instrument in the service of the state. De Callières, an early theoretician of diplomacy, tried to clarify the moral issue by stressing that diplomats should always carry out the instructions of their governments, except when they entailed doing something 'against the laws of God or of Justice', which, in his time, meant that they should not instigate assassinations nor use their diplomatic immunity to encourage revolutionaries against the sovereign to whom they were accredited.[19] Thus in addition to being a loyal servant, a diplomat should be a man of conscience. He seeks to implement policy through persuasion or compromise and by making concessions where necessary to achieve a mutually acceptable resolution of conflict. To be successful he has to operate in an atmosphere of mutual respect and trust, which implies the exercise of courtesy and patience on his part.

There can be no greater contrast between these qualities and those required of the strategist, who operates in a world of fierce and deadly competition. He sees relations between states as a matter of imposing one's will on the opponent. Victory in the struggle is elevated to an end in itself. Such perceptions lead to thinking almost exclusively of gains and loss in international relations. They impute threatening and sinister designs to an opponent and place a high value on cunning, stealth and deception.

Strategy has always been the central feature of the military art since the days of Sun Tzu, an early exponent of the skill in achieving objectives with the least amount of physical violence.[20] Once attempts at a peaceful resolution of conflict had failed, the statesman turned to the military commander, or himself became the military commander who formulated the plans and executed them in order to achieve the objectives which could not be realised by other means. But the meaning of strategy has been diluted in our time: 'It is the element of force which distinguishes "strategy" from the purposeful planning in other branches of human activity . . .'[21] The present confusion between foreign policy and strategy, and between the functions of the diplomat and the strategist has its roots in different conceptions of international politics.

Different Philosophies of International Relations

The difference between the current strategic conception of diplomacy and other ideas about its functions is illustrated by two quotations. The first is taken from a chapter on 'New Techniques in Diplomacy' by Livingston Merchant in The Dimensions of Diplomacy, edited by E.A.J. Johnson:

We do in our (United States') diplomacy, I believe, understand the fundamental role of power in relations between states, . . . We do have Jefferson's 'decent respect for the opinion of mankind'. But we must never forget that it is on sheer power – governed by wisdom and restraint – that the continuance of our civilisation now depends, . . .[22]

The second is from Maurice Pearton, *The Knowledgeable State* in which he defines the purpose of diplomacy as:

The continuous attempt to define and settle the problems arising between states by rational negotiation within agreed rules. It therefore aims at *creating and sustaining confidence and resorts to compromise.* [emphasis added][23]

Merchant's view is descended from Machiavelli's general theory that for the ruler the safety and interests of the state take precedence over all other considerations. He singled out power as the principal if not the sole objective of politics and regarded hostility as a 'natural' propensity of states:

. . . the natural hatred which neighbouring princes and neighbouring republics have for one another; which, in turn, is occasioned by the ambition which moves states to dominate one another, and by their jealousy . . .[24]

His idea of inter-state relations was carried forward by Hobbes, whose philosophy reflected the anarchical rise of the modern European state system. The distinctive Hobbesian contribution lay in the emphasis on science and knowledge as means to power rather than as ends in themselves.[25] This fits very well with the contemporary emphasis on the scientific and, above all, rational foundations of strategic theory and practice.

Clausewitz, the father of modern strategic thinking and a diplomat manqué [26], accepted Machiavelli's basic rationale of statecraft and applied it to the nature, purpose, and conduct of war in the age of emerging nation-states. The state was regarded as a living entity which tries to fulfil its ambitions intelligently. It is sovereign and recognises no sovereignty above itself. National goals are the highest values and among them the survival of the nation-state is pre-eminent. Since every state aims to increase its power and can only do so at the expense of other states, conflicts are endemic in the international system. Such clashes could be resolved either by diplomacy or by war; but as resolution could not always be achieved through negotiations, it followed that war was a normal, though spasmodic, phase in inter-state relations.

Pearton's view, on the other hand, owes its inspiration to the idea of natural law as developed by Grotius. The *ius naturale* embodied the principles which should govern human conduct. Those principles were rooted in the rational and social nature of human beings and unless this was recognised and accepted by men, nothing would prevent international anarchy.

> No just equilibrium could ever be secured unless the rulers of the world realised that there were certain principles other than national expediency that must govern the policies and their acts.[27]

The philosophy behind such a view was to be developed by Immanuel Kant.

The precepts of Grotius were applied by de Callières in his handbook on the art of diplomacy. For instance, he strongly disapproved of deceit as a method because it '. . . awakes in the defeated (i.e., deceived) party a sense of irritation, a desire for vengeance, and a hatred which must remain a menace to his foe . . .' He thought menaces were always harmful:

> Success achieved by force or fraud rests on an insecure foundation; conversely, success based on reciprocal advantage gives promise of even further successes to come.[28]

This kind of approach rests on the acceptance of the idea of a formal equality of states that implies something more than power and the pursuit of national interest as the motor of international relations. The approach of the strategist, on the other hand, is based on the assumption of the natural inequality of states which are constantly struggling to survive and assert themselves, a condition underwritten by periodic trials of strength.

The quotations from Merchant and Pearton reveal divergent ideas about the purpose of diplomacy. Merchant emphasises the power-centred approach, while Pearton stresses the conciliatory approach. Both would agree, however, that it is preferable to settle conflict through a process of negotiation, persuasion and mutual understanding than by the resort to force.

The Rise of Strategic Thinking

The rise of strategic thinking and its spread from the narrow confines of military operations into other areas of human activity did not begin in 1945. The strategic method of handling problems stems from the emergence of modern military institutions in the nineteenth century and is intimately bound up with the rise of the industrial nation-state. Indeed, the military establishment became the first modern organisation and as such served as a role model. Mass armies preceded mass production in factories employing large numbers of workers; the military staff college preceded the business school; the Schlieffen Plan preceded the Marshall Plan. Conscription played its part in making the people aware of the importance of strategy and its relation to tactical manoeuvre. Compulsory military service in Meiji Japan, for instance, had the unintended side-effect of enabling the tenant movement of the early years of this century to formulate and carry out detailed 'battle plans'.[29]

The requirements of total war brought the military into all spheres of civilian life. It penetrated industry, technology, and education, encouraging the spread of military values. Whether total war spawned totalitarian philosophies or not, the rise of Communism, Fascism, and National Socialism further encouraged the domination of strategic thinking in international relations. It was a characteristic of Marxism-Leninism to view social relations in confrontational terms. The doctrine injected 'unusually strong hostility and suspicion into Soviet policy-making' and there was no distinction between war and peace. The correct calculation of the correlation of forces and the criteria of risk, cost and gain were systematically applied to political affairs.[30] Totalitarian philosophies in general reject the idea of compromise, except as a tactical manoeuvre. The sole objective remains the total defeat of the enemy.

Until the Second World War, the military often overstepped the boundary between their proper sphere of activity and that which belonged to the civilian domain. The process of penetration was reversed after 1945 under the influence of technological developments, especially nuclear weapons. Politicians, technologists and administrators pursued 'strategies' which promoted pure and applied nuclear research in the civilian sphere with the intention of using it for military purposes. The French nuclear energy programme was a good example of this approach. The growth of dual-purpose technologies, particularly in electronics, has blurred further the distinction between the civilian and the military.

Most significant has been the involvement of civilians in military planning and the formulation of strategy. In the first 15 years after the war, all but one of the major departures of American policy as regards nuclear weapons were due to scientists and not professional soldiers.[31] Public discussion of nuclear strategy, both in its deterrent and its war-fighting role, has been largely conducted by civilians: academics, economists, scientists, technologists, bureaucrats, journalists, philosophers and theologians. The indirect effect has been to encourage adversarial and confrontational attitudes in international relations. They were seen primarily as relations between opponents. The application of game theory has strengthened the view that the competitive relationship is the norm in intercourse between states.

We might sum up what has just been described by saying that the period before 1945 was marked by a passive adoption of strategic thinking as a consequence of the expanding military demands on society. In contrast, the post-1945 era has been marked by the active adoption of strategic thinking under the influence of nuclear armament and the doctrines associated with it.

The growing impact of strategic thinking on foreign policy, with its stress on punishing or vanquishing the enemy is illustrated by the conduct of the victors in three great wars. After the Napoleonic Wars it took only three years before France was admitted as a full and active member of the Concert of Powers at the Congress of Aix-la-Chapelle. Its behaviour had been regarded as an aberration and it was always assumed that it would return to its place as a major actor on the European stage. At the end of the First World War, the terms of the Treaty of Versailles were a demonstration of total victory and designed to inflict punishment on the vanquished. The settlement failed because of indecision and disunity among the allies in the face of German rancour. In the Second World War, the decision to impose unconditional surrender on the enemy marked the triumph of the strategic over the political objective. The opponent was given no choice to negotiate the re-establishment of peaceful relations, even if there were to be a change of regime from within. An attitude which was well illustrated by Churchill's response to the news of the attempted overthrow of Hitler in July 1944.[32] Surrender and not an armistice or negotiation was to be the outcome of defeat.

The culmination of the encroachment of strategy, the instrument of war, on diplomacy, the instrument of peaceful intercourse, came during the so-called cold war – a term used to describe a relationship between states which retained the normal diplomatic practices of peacetime in an atmosphere of frozen hostility. The osmosis between strategy and diplomacy is described in the following extracts from an essay written by Walt Rostow, a leading American policymaker in the early 1960s:

. . . Blessedly, the nation is not at war; but there is a sense in which the Department of State is at war. We are engaged in vital activities on many active fronts. The task is not, therefore, to make the equivalent of contingency plans for certain abstract future circumstances; the task is to conceive of specific objectives in particular theaters of activity to determine how to move forward towards those objectives under rapidly changing operational circumstances.

As in active warfare, it is important for foreign policy to have lucid, long-run objectives, defined with sufficient precision to serve as touchstones for operational decisions. One needs a doctrine in foreign policy as in war.

One of the most important developments within the Policy Planning Council [of the Department of State] in recent years has been the expansion of work done with the military and in politico-military planning in its widest sense. This development stems from a widely shared perception; namely, that the traditional sharp distinction between diplomacy and the application of military power has ended.

. . . This has resulted in an intensification of contact and co-operation between the Department of State and the Pentagon quite unprecedented in our history; a co-operation more intimate, even, than during the Second World War or the Korean War.

We seek, in short, to contribute to the osmotic relation between the military and civilian branches of the government which our problems demand for as far ahead as any of us can peer.[33]

These lines were written on the eve of the major American involvement in Vietnam, which marked the triumph of the strategic perspective in foreign policy, with disastrous results. Note that foreign policy in peacetime is to be conducted like operations in war. One talks of 'fronts' and 'theatres' of activity and of moving forward towards objectives 'under rapidly changing operational circumstances'. Just as strategy requires doctrine, so does foreign policy.[34] The language used in describing both the objectives and the methods of foreign policy is indistinguishable from the objectives and methods of strategy.

This is made explicit when Rostow asserts that 'the traditional sharp distinction between diplomacy and the application of military power has ended'. Hence the virtual merging of the functions of the government departments which are responsible for the conduct of foreign and defence policies. The intimacy of the co-operation between the State Department and the Pentagon exceeds even the intimacy to be expected in time of war. As examples of this kind of collaboration, Rostow cites the fact that the two military members of the Policy Planning Council were indistinguishable from the others, except for their expertise, and that some of the civilian members had worked over long periods of time on Pentagon projects.[35]

In brief, the theoretical bases of strategy and the functions of the professional strategist are no longer to be distinguished from the theoretical foundations of diplomacy and the functions of the professional diplomat. The technological and ideological environment of the post-war era spurred the 'osmotic relation between the military and civilian branches of the government'. That relationship was rooted in the power-centred approach to international politics, which regards the balance of power as the essential objective of state policy for those who want to retain the *status quo*. The revisionists who seek to alter the established order do not share this concept, but nonetheless accept the power-centred approach. Both attribute the most important role in the achievement of their objectives to the military. This view was articulated by Henry Kissinger:

> Throughout history the political influence of nations has been roughly correlative to their military power. . . . diplomatic skill could augment but never substitute for military strength. In the final reckoning weakness has invariably tempted aggression and impotence brings abdication of policy in its train. Some lesser countries have played significant roles on the world scale for brief periods, but only when they were acting in the secure framework of an international equilibrium. The balance of power, . . . has, in fact, been the precondition of peace.[36]

Leaving aside the question whether the balance of power has ever done anything more than keep the peace for relatively brief periods in history and that it has invariably been challenged by those dissatisfied with the *status quo* – a challenge that often ended in war – Kissinger's argument firmly places diplomatic skill and, by implication, the objectives of diplomacy in a position subordinate to military strength and, again by implication, the objectives of strategy.

Redressing the Balance

The end of the cold war in Europe and the beginning of an era of profound change in its political and ideological structures has undermined the rationale for the dominance of strategic thinking in the conduct of international relations. All of a sudden, the assumptions underlying the Atlantic Alliance have lost their importance. Nuclear weapons and strategy, which have for so long set the agenda for intra-alliance relations and its posture towards the Soviet Union, have been pushed into the background. The arguments over short-range nuclear weapons, over first use, over flexible response and forward defence have largely lost their meaning. The difficulty of breaking free from their stranglehold over the conduct of foreign policy is manifest when we look at British, French and, to a lesser extent, American reactions to events since 1989 as the Socialist bloc and then the Soviet Union itself collapsed.

Because of the overriding importance of the military dimension in their European policies, the NATO allies were not only slow to respond to the dramatic changes in Eastern Europe and the Soviet Union but were also unable to develop innovative and imaginative policies to deal with the revolutionary transformation. This was not only due to an understandable and sensible caution and to the problem of reaching consensus among 16 states of differing size, strength and interests. It was also due to the paralysing grip of nuclear armament and nuclear strategic theories on the policies of key members of the Alliance.

De Gaulle had always seen the independent French nuclear force as a tool, among other tools, with which to achieve his foreign policy objectives. Whatever one may think of them and the assumptions that they revealed, nuclear armament and strategy remained adjuncts to the conduct of external relations. However, as French nuclear armament developed and became more sophisticated, his successors had to pay attention to the need to formulate a precise strategic doctrine for its use. The acquisition of so-called 'tactical' nuclear weapons had the ironic effect of pushing France towards a *de facto* reintegration into the Alliance structure, especially through its relations with Germany. The subsequent requirement of co-ordination with the German strategic posture and general collaboration with the allies in central Europe circumscribed the room for manoeuvre by an independent foreign policy.

The events of 1989 made Germany the pace-setter of Western policy, a situation which the possession of a French nuclear armament had been designed to avoid. Furthermore, the challenges posed by Soviet arms control and disarmament initiatives paralysed French policy, whose main purpose became the preservation of the *Force de Dissuasion Nationale*. It was the French President of the European Community's Commission, and not the French Foreign Minister, who took initiatives in the construction of the new Europe.

British hesitancy and immobilism in the face of upheavals in Eastern Europe were also influenced by a concern over the national nuclear deterrent. Mrs Thatcher's devotion to NATO, her unwillingness to think of alternative security structures and her insistence that the modernisation of short-range nuclear weapons must continue were dictated more by anxieties over the future of Britain's nuclear force than by residual anxieties about the Soviet Union. The prospect that the United States might cut off the *Trident* missile programme in a START deal with the Soviet Union threatened the foundations of Britain's defence posture. The United States was no less hamstrung in its initial responses to the dramatic changes in Europe. The primacy of strategic considerations in its foreign policy left it unprepared in the face of a complete change in the international environment.

The Soviet Union had, of course, been similarly affected in the past. For decades, especially under Brezhnev, military/strategic considerations had driven its external policy and it was only the weakness of the socio-economic system which forced it to reassess the priorities and methods of its foreign policy, so that Mr Shevardnadze could say:

A country's foreign policy is viable only when it bases itself on the law, on convictions, on compatible interests and targets, on co-operation and interaction. The policy of using military power to underpin diplomacy always drove states to political bankruptcy or catastrophe. Great empires collapsed, while states which have practically no armed forces flourish.

Foreign policy can only achieve limited objectives . . .

It is time we understood that neither socialism, nor friendship, nor good neighbourliness, nor respect can rely on bayonets, tanks, and bloodshed. Relations with any country must be built on mutual interests, mutual advantage, on the principle of free choice.[37]

The strategic jargon lingers, as in the use of the word 'targets', and it could be argued that the rhetoric is not so different from the rhetoric of those who claimed that a strong military posture and reliance on the deterrent were the necessary preconditions of peace and the triumph of Socialism. There is a hint of the Paul Kennedy thesis, developed in his book *The Rise and Fall of the Great Powers*,[38] in the reasons for the collapse of great empires and an oblique reference to new forms of power which rely on economic strength, no doubt with Japan and Germany in mind. But there is also a recognition of other, non-strategic objectives of foreign policy and diplomacy: the search for co-operation; mutual interests and mutual advantage; and an awareness that free choice rather than compulsion is a sounder basis on which to build more durable and friendly international relations.

All this is not to argue that it only requires awareness of these truths on the part of political leaders to make them reality or that the military dimension of national policy has ceased to have any significance. One of the difficulties of any fundamental reorientation of security policy lies in the enormous financial, material and intellectual investment in armaments, especially nuclear weaponry. Another obstacle is the need for prudence. No one can foretell the outcome of revolutionary change which is still under way and may be in its early stages, particularly in the former Soviet Union. Communist domination may have passed into history, but a resurgent, xenophobic expansionist Russia, still in possession of a mighty armoury, could pose one day a new threat to its neighbours. It would be irresponsible and foolish for governments to discard all means of defence in the light of such uncertainties. Endemic violence in the Third World and the alarming spread of the most sophisticated weapons in unstable regions form a third obstacle to reduced reliance on the military instrument in foreign policy.

Nonetheless, the current transformation of the international system offers an opportunity to break the hold of strategic thinking on the conduct of external relations. One step towards the restoration of other values of diplomacy would include the replacement of the objective of *victory* over the other party with the objective of *mutual adjustment* to accommodate conflicting interests.

Another step would involve the deliberate identification of *shared interests* as a preliminary to international negotiations. Such an exercise already exists in the field of arms control where there is a commonly agreed objective of preventing the outbreak of war through accident, misunderstanding or miscalculation. Wider issues, such as the creation of a more stable world economy, measures for handling the international debt problem, transnational terrorism, mass migrations, and protection of the environment are the natural bases for the recognition of shared interests. Work on this aspect of inter-state relations would have the effect of increasing the importance of policy-planning and research departments in foreign ministries to counter the tendency towards short-term, *ad hoc* operations that govern most foreign policies. Such approaches would also require the abandoning of the habit of thinking in absolute terms, of seeing the other side in negotiations as the opponent or enemy. During the cold war, this confrontational view coloured the rhetoric on both sides, although in practice the actual dialogue was governed by the mutual but unspoken acceptance of common interests.

This leads to another step: the reinstatement of the traditional practices of courtesy, patience and listening in the negotiating process. Elementary and obvious requirements as they may be, they would emphasise the quality of mutual respect, however great the differences and contentions. The step may be simple, but the obstacles are formidable for two reasons. One has to do with the desire of the media to present international encounters in terms of confrontation and conflict, not only reinforcing the concept of international relations as a game of strategy, but also encouraging leaders to take a confrontational attitude with an eye to their image at home. A notable exception so far has been the posture of Japanese prime ministers, where the requirements of popularity at home demand the image of an important international figure, but certainly not one of the tough guy ready to use force.

The other obstacle is the popular expectation raised by the practice of summitry and the sense of failure when agreement is not reached at these highly publicised encounters. It would be necessary, therefore, to dampen public expectations and to place greater emphasis on confidential and private diplomacy.

It is the supreme paradox that the cold war and the influence of nuclear armouries on policy have not only led to foreign policies dominated by strategic thinking, but have also opened the way to its replacement by other approaches to the conduct of inter-state relations.

Conditions of modern warfare have shifted the emphasis from the ability to fight a war successfully to war avoidance through crisis management. Robert McNamara's dictum that 'Today there is no longer any such thing as military strategy; there is only crisis management',[39] is now widely accepted. If we look at the conditions for successful crisis management, we note that many of them, though applied in a strategic context, apply equally to the requirements of a successful, non-strategically-orientated diplomacy. They include: firm civilian control over all aspects of military activity; the co-ordination of diplomatic and military moves; military gestures to be confined to demonstrations of resolve and to be appropriate to limited objectives; avoidance of provocative deployments; and, most important, that all activity should indicate a desire to negotiate and that only those options that leave the other party an opportunity to escape an impasse and that are compatible with its fundamental interests should be employed. The Cuban missile crisis of 1962 is an example where crisis management resulted in accommodation rather than victory or defeat. Moreover, the outcome had a positive effect and led to an improvement in the management of superpower relations which continued and survived all subsequent crises.

The generally recognised need for crisis management has been reinforced by the technological revolution that is currently sweeping the world, by the ever more pressing demands of economic interdependence, and by the urgency of measures to protect the global environment. One might go further. It is essential to establish the primacy of basic good will, the search for compromise, the establishment of mutual respect and trust as objectives of diplomacy if there is to be any progress towards a more integrated world system in which inter-state relations rest on consent rather than coercion.

Military strength and strategic analysis have always been elements in the conduct of foreign policy, but the first task of its principal instrument, diplomacy, is to seek the peaceful adjustment of relations with other states. That requires a certain cast of mind and special skills which are not the same as those required of a strategist.

2

Security in a New Age?

Barrie Paskins

How portentous should our thinking be as we look forward towards the new millennium? Are we to expect business as usual, or changes which are so far-reaching as to warrant talk of a 'new age'? What we currently term the ending of the cold war brings with it so many obvious discontinuities that we can scarcely avoid raising the question of whether we are entering a new age. And though it is far too early for anyone to answer the question, it may be timely to consider what may come to be most important in determining an answer. Hence the title ends with a question mark. Must we locate our thinking about security henceforth within the context of a new age? The question is a good one and I intend to sketch how the issue might be conceptualised.

The Nature of Security

What kind of thing is security? Security is a value, one among a number of ill-assorted and vitally important values. Insecurity is a '*dis*value', a bad thing, one among a number of evils to which we are unavoidably averse. We want security, and we fear and loathe and shun insecurity. There is good reason for this in human nature. As individuals and in our collective existence we are vulnerable to one another in a great variety of ways. We and those we love and that which we cherish can readily be destroyed, damaged, enslaved, or stolen. Human history is full of examples, and there is no known way of guaranteeing ourselves immunity in future from the familiar travails of vulnerability. To the extent that we have security, there are limits to our vulnerability: things that we can count on to enable us to exist and to love and cherish without immediate destruction or impending catastrophe. Objective insecurity is the lack of such protection.

Human beings differ considerably in what they love and cherish. Within different societies honour, wealth, sanctity, love of my neighbour, beauty, knowledge, and so on, are prized and misprized to

17

differing extents, and within a given society different individuals and different groups may have different objects of affection. What is virtually universal is the vulnerability, and the consequent concern with security and insecurity. Vulnerable beings such as ourselves should be able to understand one another's anxiety about security even if we are unwilling to see the point of another's loving and cherishing. 'I don't understand what she sees in him', we might say, 'but I understand her jealousy all too well', or 'I don't see why they are concerned about honour, but I cannot fail to comprehend their reasons for surrounding such a holy of holies with formidable security systems.' To do so is characteristic of our loving and vulnerable species. It can happen that the life of an individual goes so drastically wrong that, while he or she is in some sense rational, nevertheless there is nothing that we can recognise as being the object of his or her love. If such a person is, as is quite likely, immured in all-consuming melancholy and indifference then his or her condition will be pitiful but without any special bearing upon our understanding of security. But it can also happen, if only in very rare cases, that such a person, loving nothing, is nevertheless full of diabolical energy, a profoundly destructive genius consisting of all hate and no love. Erich Fromm in his book *The Anatomy of Human Destructiveness* seeks to characterise and explain this extreme human type, and to exemplify it in the characters of Hitler and Stalin. [1] If Fromm is right, then individuals who are entirely devoid of love may be of the utmost importance to the student of security, for nothing can be more vital than to understand, the better to oppose, the coming to power and continuance in office of such monsters of iniquity.

But it would be a mistake to infer that the unloving individual is a good focus for our thoughts when we try to make clear to ourselves what security is. Hitler and Stalin came to power and were suffered to rule by people whose loves were many, who cherished many things, including much of great value; the question of how these affectionate beings allowed themselves to be dominated by scarcely human creatures is at least as vital as the inner life and outward exploits of their leaders. To understand Stalinism and the Third Reich, we need not so much an entrée into the heart and mind of the supreme villain as to comprehend his hold upon beings much like ourselves. The practical reason is that the psychopath is a problem of security rather than of criminology or medicine only to the extent that he, or she, is able to mobilise the energies of many and various human beings. The deeper, contemplative reason is that we cannot know ourselves for what we are unless we can grasp what we, individually and in our several collective identities, would have been capable of both for good and evil if exposed to the mesmeric psychopath. It is nowhere more important than in strategic studies to remember that the proper study of mankind is man – man as distinct from the monster, though of course, including the female of the species.

I am claiming here that security is in a certain sense an objective value. The objectivity derives from human nature. Because we love and cherish, we human beings need and prize security, and shun insecurity. Even if I cannot understand why you love as you do, I cannot fail to understand that you, as a loving being, have security concerns. And this applies to collective entities such as states as well as to individuals, because states consist largely of beings such as ourselves even if they are sometimes dominated by monsters who are scarcely human.

To assert that security is in this sense an objective value is not to imply that there is some measure of security which we ought to be able to count on discovering; for example, in order to answer the famous question of 'how much is enough?' for deterrence. On the contrary, there is good reason to believe that the very idea of such a measure is absurd. Security is one among a number of values. We unavoidably desire not only security for our people but also health, wealth, education and all the other good things for which, as common goods, it is proper for the state to raise taxes and to create institutions. The security budget must compete with health, education and the rest. And there are hard choices always to be made about where to set the level of taxation, and where to draw a line between public and private initiative, accumulation and expenditure. We have here a number of values – security, health, education, private liberty, public spirit – and a moment's reflection on how each of these fits into our lives should suffice to indicate that it would be very surprising indeed if these values were commensurable, that is, could be brought under one common measure. Such values are so obviously plural that one would require a most spectacular feat of applied mathematics to be persuaded that they could be measured one against another; hence it is no surprise that there is no known common measure, and that decisions between such values are political rather than technical. It should be no surprise, and assuredly not a basis for reproach, if arms control negotiators are unable to agree on measures of how much is enough in dealings between mutually mistrustful states when we know full well that security, though an objective value, is not a value susceptible of measurement even within the most cohesive of states, or the fondest of families.

How are we to think about security if we cannot measure it? I suggest that a threefold distinction may be helpful. I incline to distinguish, first, technical; second, political; and third, moral and spiritual factors in our thinking about security. The problem of arms control verification furnishes a convenient example. Discussions of verification often involve purely technical questions, such as concern the feasibility of distinguishing an earthquake from an underground test explosion. Political questions are unavoidable: will or can the US Congress co-operate with a certain proposed substantive arms control agreement? What kind of risks can or should a country's political leadership be prepared to take in the interest of confidence-building? Finally there is a kind of question which I shall call 'moral/spiritual': what sorts of risk should we, in all conscience, be prepared to take, or to refuse to take, for the sake of justice and peace?

As this example illustrates, political factors shade-off at one end into the technical and at other into the moral/spiritual domain. A political question of an almost entirely technical kind might be concerned with how Congress can be persuaded to block a certain proposal. A geologist who decides to emphasise some, rather than other, technical possibilities in support of the Scientists Against Nuclear Arms organisation (SANA) or the Committee on the Present Danger is mixing the purely technical with the characteristically political, and why not so long as no one is deceived? At the other end of the political spectrum is a shading-off from a political question about what risks the President may legitimately run to a moral/spiritual question about the risks which we all, in conscience, must be prepared to take.

Philosophising about Security in a New Age

I propose to organise my analysis about the new age which may be dawning in terms of a tripartite division between the technical, the political, and the moral/spiritual. The technical shades into the political which in turn shades into the moral/spiritual.

Must we expect our thinking about security in the 1990s and beyond to be located within a context which is so radically altered as to warrant talk of a new age? No one doubts that new technical challenges are coming which will require and stimulate new responses. An obvious, and obviously far-reaching, example is environmental pollution, consideration of which is very much to my purpose because some believe that this technical stimulus requires a response which is as much moral/spiritual as it is technical.

The stimulus comes from the scientific discovery that human activities which have been supposed to be innocent and even virtuous are having the unintended effect of poisoning our environment, of damaging the material preconditions of human survival, let alone human prosperity. This discovery is associated in many minds, and more especially in the feelings of many people, with anguish at the accelerating extinction of animal and plant species, and the destruction of long-cherished or fascinating landscapes.

The exact details of this new threat to our security are of great practical importance, but are not our concern here. Having already noticed that security is an objective but not measurable value, we should be no more puzzled that scientists disagree about the exact details of global warming than that there is controversy in every area of arms control verification, even the most narrowly technical. What I wish to dwell upon is the *kind* of issue that we are presented with by the urgent threat of ecological disaster.

The scientists have alerted us all to this new danger. They have subjected us to a novel, originally technical, stimulus. No one doubts that the response needs to be at least partly technical, and only the most pessimistic doubt that something of the kind, however inadequate, will be forthcoming. We need to avoid the use of certain chemicals, and how to do so is a technical problem. We probably need to use energy resources less wastefully, and in ways that liberate less heat and other waste products into the atmosphere – another technical problem. But it is not these technical matters that cause ecology to have an important place in any attempt to envisage a new security agenda. It is the carry-over into politics, and into the moral/spiritual domain, that converts a technical stimulus into the demand for some for a kind of response which would assuredly warrant talk of a new age.

Let me sketch the kind of radical position that I have in mind. The 'radical ecologist', as I shall call him or her, maintains that we must alter fundamentally our relationship with nature, as follows: 'our civilisation is built upon the exploitation of nature', the radical ecologist would say, 'our mastery of nature has now gone so far that we are in danger of destroying the preconditions of human life, and *a fortiori* of human prosperity. We need to change very quickly to a far less exclusive, less parochial perspective. We must think hard and constantly and systematically about the rights of future generations, and of other species that we are driving to extinction. Everything that we do must be scrutinised from an ecological perspective. Nuclear deterrence theory must take account of nuclear winter. Analysis of the Gulf War of 1990–91 must not lose sight of the global environmental impact of that conflict in the phenomenon of hundreds of burning oil wells. The idea that security can be sought through economic growth and the appeasement of the poor's resentment by allowing them a share of the benefits of growth must be re-examined to determine whether the planet can stand such rapacious human demands. Humanity is an inadequate basis for the new ethic because it is a characteristic product of man's tyranny over nature, which needs to be replaced by something gentler and more modest. We are to be the stewards not the lords of creation. Justice and peace are inseparable from the integrity of creation, sustainable economic growth or stasis or retreat.'

I have granted one important point to such people as this ecological radical in the way that I have divided the spectrum of our thinking about security. I distinguished the technical, the political, and what I called the moral/spiritual. The word 'moral' alone would not suffice, because there are reasons for doubting that any exclusively moral characterisation of that end of the spectrum would be adequate to bring out what may be at stake. The ecological radical puts a finger on the essential point when he or she contends that we need to regard nature in a quite new spirit, of humility and contrition and harmony-seeking. I shall criticise the views which I have attributed to the ecological radical; but on this point I believe him or her to be entirely correct. When we speak of 'morality' we very often have in mind a given set of rules or principles which leap to mind whenever conscience speaks within us. As we look forward towards the new millennium it is imperative that we consider not only morality in this sense of rules or principles but also the spirit in which we approach the whole business of living, the spirit in which we steer between the demands of conscience and necessity. The spiritual – that is, the spirit in which we live – is as essential as the more narrowly moral when we move from the technical through the political to the other end of the spectrum. About that I agree with the ecological radical.

But let us move to the criticism. Does the radical ecologist identify correctly the reasons why we need to re-examine the moral/spiritual dimension? Is the direction in which he or she proposes to go the right one? I think not. This ecologist maintains that our existing spiritual, moral and intellectual resources are inadequate. But is our sense of humanity incapable of grasping what we are invited to call the rights of future generations? No, it is not. We are perfectly capable of realising that pollution will adversely affect our children, and our children's children, and so on through the ages; and of being moved by the plight of beings who are made precious to us by being, like us, human parents and human children. And if there are any who cannot be moved by such an appeal to the heart, it is in practice bizarre, and on reflection irrational, to suppose that an inevitably controversial exposition of the supposed rights of future generations could accomplish what love cannot. If poisoning babies is not in itself unthinkable, as of course it is, then the basis for a doctrine of human rights is lacking.

The point is equally clear as regards animals. 'Do dolphins have rights?' is a difficult question that plunges one immediately into perplexity. But look at a television programme by David

Attenborough or David Bellamy and what do you see? You see creatures so wondrous that it would be unthinkable to destroy them gratuitously. Attenborough and his team enable one to look upon the natural world, or rather upon members of some other species, with the eyes of love, eyes to which conservation is as natural, and exploitation as inconceivable, as it is natural for any lover to cherish the beloved.

This is available within our existing humanity, indeed depends upon it. It is no accident that Attenborough is so often in the picture, for it is in part his infectious love that enables the rest of us to see the dolphins and the rest for what they are, lovable creatures whose survival and prosperity we, of course, desire when once we have seen them for what they are. There is no reason to believe that a new morality or a new spirit will add any strength whatever to the urgent concern we already feel for future generations and for the members of some endangered species.

These emotional resources which are readily available to us without any revolution in our morals or spirit do not, of course, suffice to bring about all that needs to be done. And comment is undoubtedly required on the fact that many are attracted by such positions as that of the radical ecologist because the promptings of our hearts seem so insufficient to the task that is set before us by, let us remember, those very promptings. It is the demands of love that make us feel how powerless we are, and prod us towards desiring a new, more efficacious philosophy. Before discussing this, however, I need to dwell upon certain deficiencies in what I am calling the outlook of radical ecology. That outlook urges that we require a new relationship to the whole of nature, and I see this as being a grave deficiency in it.

The question of what is meant by 'nature' could profitably occupy a long series of studies. By far the most powerful and impressive conception of nature that is available to us is that which derives from the natural sciences, from physics, chemistry and biology. According to that conception, the natural world is far older and far larger than was ever imagined by any of the ancient philosophers, save those who guessed, it seems wrongly, that time and space are infinite. It is also vastly stranger than could have been guessed in any earlier age, apparently comprising eleven dimensions and whose smallest entities have the bizarre characteristic of resembling both particles and waves. Within this strange domain, it seems, the variety of biological species arose by non-purposive chemical processes, by the operation of natural selection upon genetic mutation. Everything that is natural within and around us is so by being part of this totally unexpected discovery of applied mathematics.

This is what nature is, and it is to this that the radical ecologist would have us change our attitude. But what is that attitude? It can only be one of astonishment, wonder, perplexity. To imagine that we could be masters of nature is absurd – we will not be here long enough. We will already be gone before the stars cease to shine, long before the end.

It will be replied that this is not what the radical ecologist means by nature, that something much more ready to hand is intended. What might that be? The planet earth, perhaps? But it is unthinkable that we should lord it over the earth. Think how shallow are the deepest mines, and how little we can think of discovering directly about the earth's core. Or is it the biosphere that is intended? This is more promising since the biosphere is defined as that portion of the earth in which life can be found, and so is bound to include any part that we are able to reach. Should we revere and serve the biosphere? On reflection, it is a bizarre or chilling hypothesis. The AIDS virus and the malarial mosquito as well as the dolphin are inhabitants of the biosphere, and we cannot look upon them with the same love that David Attenborough can enable us to feel for the dolphin. Sadly, these destructive organisms need to be eradicated for the simple reason that they are such a threat to us and to our children. There are dangerous non-human species with which we can afford to live, providing the risks are not too great – wolves perhaps – though we must assuredly not under-estimate the risks to front-line human beings in calculating the risk. But there are species whose members are, alas, our natural enemies and with which we cannot live. It is them or us. To say this is not to claim dominion over the whole of nature; merely to know one's enemy.

When our minds are opened to the wondrous constitution of the malarial mosquito or the AIDS virus, we cannot but regret that we, who did not design this world, must strive to eradicate such magnificent creatures. To that extent, love finds a place even here. But if the radical ecologist is really proposing that we need to bring a new spirit to our relations with nature, he or she must surely be going further than to claim what our everyday humanity will readily agree to. When he or she tells us that it is arbitrary, tyrannical and unjust to lay such central importance upon our own kind, the claim to be distinctive must surely be that eradication programmes are repugnant in principle, that preservation of the AIDS virus is the same sort of thing as conserving the dear dolphin. I submit that this is bizarre if it is merely asserted, and chilling if it is meant seriously – if the proposer is so far forgetting him- or herself – as to speak as though it were arbitrary to distinguish between a baby and the micro-organism which is lethal to it.

There are powerful forces in our culture which encourage one to interpret the point at which I have now arrived in a manner to which I am resistant. We tend to think that philosophies are subjective, and that if I disagree with the radical ecologist then the conversation is the kind of thing that can go on indefinitely without any of the kinds of conclusive outcome that should interest anyone but the parties to the immediate debate. My way of resisting this general belief at this particular point is by way of remembering why so many people nowadays take seriously something like the position of the radical ecologist. If we can become clear about this, we should be better equipped to determine whether it can count as a refutation of radical ecology that it involves drawing no significant difference between a baby and the AIDS virus.

Why is the radical ecologist taken so seriously? First, there is the stimulus from the scientists, the threat to our security and the plea to the heart on behalf of the dolphins. Secondly, I believe, there is a deep mistrust of politics. And thirdly, there is a manipulative attitude to the activity of philosophising. The people who are most attracted by such radical positions as the one that I have outlined mistrust politics and *therefore* have a manipulative attitude to philosophy. To sustain this assertion, we must consider politics. How should we characterise the political context of any discussion of whether a new age is dawning?

I take it that no one doubts that the pollution problem is global in the sense that it can be coped with, if at all, then only by agencies that are empowered to act throughout the world. How should we conceptualise that stark fact politically? Now that the cold war is over, this question admits of a new kind of answer, which a few words of historical background will suffice to introduce. After the First World War, a new kind of purposive organization was created, with the prevention of war as its basic objective. The first such organisation was the League of Nations, a catastrophic failure. The second of this kind, the United Nations (UN), was designed in such a way as to benefit from the lessons of the League. It is a modified oligarchy. Formidable responsibilities and powers are vested in the principal states, alias the Permanent Members of the Security Council. It is for them in concert to bang heads together in order to create and preserve collective security. Their supremacy is, however, qualified by the participation of non-Permanent Members in the Security Council, by the General Assembly, and by the great variety of functions which are entrusted to the UN's Special Agencies.

One of the greatest questions with which any student of security has constantly to wrestle is that of the principal unit of analysis of political and security matters. Does the world, for example, consist principally of sovereign states, or of bureaucracies, or of economic entities of some sort, be they companies, national economies or classes? I suggest that what we call the ending of the cold war permits and perhaps even requires us to respond to this perennial question in terms that recognise the primary importance of that modified oligarchy the United Nations. Both traditional security problems, such as that of regional warfare, and new security problems, such as that of pollution, need to be conceptualised primarily, I suggest, in terms of the UN, at least in so far as we are concerned with the political, as distinct from the purely technical, at one end, and the moral/spiritual at the other end of the spectrum.

Why the UN? I suggest that we increasingly inhabit a world in which there are a few great powers and a great many truly global problems, stimuli to which an adequate response will be possible only through the active participation of these powers to the point at which these states find their very identity to be inseparably bound up with the quality of their participation in this system. One of the many things that can be meant by 'sovereignty' is that the great powers are able to identify themselves primarily in ways that we might call 'autarchic', so that the United States might be identified primarily through its domestic institutions, the relation between its citizens and their land, and the new world of innocence and liberty that this separate place represents in the old world – a refuge, an escape, something isolated and separate. What I want to suggest is that the age we are entering is not like that because the great powers, most especially the great powers, are coming to be identified for all sorts of reasons by the nature and quality of their active participation in a global system whose principal institutional expression is the United Nations. I shall try to explain more fully below one aspect of what I mean by this.

For the moment I want to relate this notion of the UN as the principal unit of politics to my discussion of the radical ecologist, whom I have described as despairing of conventional politics, and of wanting a new philosophy because he or she despairs of conventional politics.

During the cold war, the UN was immobilised by the mutual hostility of the two most important great powers, so that it was natural that anyone whose concerns were global, in the sense that the radical ecologist's concerns are global, should despair of conventional politics. Those concerns demand a vibrantly active and creative UN, and the reality was so obviously and inevitably different. Now the United Nations system has a significantly greater potential, but we are not yet hearing from such people as my radical ecologist what this might mean because the old habits die hard – the old despair of politics, the old compensatory desire for a new philosophy.

The present political moment is one of radical political uncertainty and one of its most striking characteristics is the almost total lack of new political ideas. What I am suggesting is that one of the forms that such ideas might and should take is that people such as my radical ecologist should re-think their concerns in terms of the modified oligarchy of the United Nations system, a system which is carrying us beyond the sterile old polarity between sovereignty and world government towards a position in which the most important states find their identity in the quality of their leadership in matters which they are unable to define exclusively on their own terms. Can the great powers become essentially committed, to the core of their being, to the task of leadership in the common interest over matters of global concern, such as pollution? I do not know, and one of the reasons why none of us knows is that this very interesting and potentially creative question has not yet been subjected to study and advocacy by people in whom care for the common interest is combined with political ambition, ability and vision.

Thus I should like the ecological campaigner to concentrate on moulding his or her concerns into the form of international politics. I want to hear hard questions addressed and clarified, such as what powers for intervention might be granted to the UN or its Permanent Members for the control of pollution, as well as tough-minded expositions of who might be expected to pay? How, for example, would it be if the costs of controlling and reducing pollution were levied upon UN members in proportion to the pollution they produce as measured by an independent agency? Would that uselessly impoverish the already poor? Would such an agency be made totally dependent by such a rule on a principal pay-master who would be certain to fix the pollution measurement in such a way as to doom us all to eco-disaster? There is surely scope for a great deal of immediately relevant study in such areas.

I accused my radical ecologist of having a manipulative attitude to the activity of philosophising, and the next step in my argument is to explain what I mean by this. We live in a pragmatic age, one that tends to judge everything, even beliefs, by the pay-off, the consequences. There is a tendency in this direction even in the natural sciences. Newton supposed himself, in doing what we call physics, to be reading the mind of God. Many contemporary physicists will settle for the more modest claim that their theories are the best available way of accommodating the evidence – however outlandish, they 'seem to work'. In a pragmatic age, it is no surprise to find activists casting about for beliefs and images to serve and round out their practical activity. Beginning as a pressure group striving to emphasise the need for action against pollution, people quite naturally in our time adopt as a philosophy whatever intellectual positions seem best fitted to direct attention and to motivate action in the ways that they desire. This is not manipulation from without, not mere propaganda, for ours is a time in which it is respectable to judge even theories of nature on the basis that they 'seem to work'. What more natural than that a person or group should embrace whatever beliefs and images 'seem to work' for the protection of the environment. Natural though it has come to be, this tendency is pernicious. In arguing this, we come at last to the sense in which I believe that we may indeed be entering a new age.

A New Age

My conclusion that a new age may, indeed, be dawning is arrived at in two stages. First, I shall offer an analysis of pragmatism in general. Secondly, at greater length, I shall suggest a historical context for the rethinking of our attitudes both to philosophy and to security.

First, of pragmatism in general there is a good and powerful reason why so many (though by no means all) natural scientists are pragmatic these days in their attitude to scientific theory. Newton, as we have mentioned, supposed himself in his physics to be reading the mind of God. As late as the end of the eighteenth century, it still made sense for the greatest of thinkers, for instance Kant, to believe that the science of nature was progressive in a peculiarly simple way. Kant assumed that the geometry developed by the ancient Greeks was the one true geometry, that the physics of Newton was the one true physics, and that the progress of science consisted in the uncovering of further verities which would stay in place as geometry and Newtonian physics were expected to do. The problem for Kant's philosophy of nature was to explain how this was possible.

Kant turned out to be wrong. It turned out that the geometry required for Einstein's physics was not that of Euclid. It was discovered that Newton's physics was not the last word, but a wondrously close approximation on which we can improve for reasons that we can, up to a point, explain. The most immovable-seeming verities collapsed without disclosing deeper immobiles. What came to light lower down was the bizarre and arbitrary-seeming shambles of relativity and quantum theory, which we still do not know how to combine. Small wonder that Newton's confidence of being able to read the mind of God as inscribed in nature should give way to a merely pragmatic acceptance of the inconclusive findings of current theory.

Further support for pragmatism has come from biology. The natural sciences have progressed so far in the direction of being able to understand biological phenomena in terms of underlying chemical and physical processes that it no longer seems surprising that the world might be other than the best efforts of the human mind can disclose. If all adaptations of all species are to be explained in terms of their survival value, then the noble belief that the highest aim of the human mind is truth is eroded into the doctrine that a belief is to be accepted to the extent that it works, that it is conducive to survival. Thus there is much in the natural sciences which encourages pragmatism. So then, to the historical context of the argument.

The twentieth century is over. It was short, enduring only from 1914 to 1989, from Sarajevo to the pulling-down of the Berlin Wall. But lest anyone suppose me to imagine that the *Zeitgeist* cannot count, let me hasten to agree that this short century was the latter part of a larger period of exactly 200 years, from the French Revolution to the end of the cold war. This period might be termed 'the secular age', to emphasise one of its leading characteristics, for this was the age in which a determined effort was made to locate human life exclusively in this world, the natural world, the only world of which we know. This was the time in which the older belief in a supernatural realm enclosing the natural world was jettisoned. It was the time in which the best and worst of men and women were encouraged to identify their individual and collective well-being in this world alone, and to abandon once and for all the old idea that this life is short compared with the life to come.

At the beginning of the secular age, this seemed a liberating and encouraging development. By concentrating on what we could expect to know, by unmasking superstition and freeing ourselves of the opiate of servile dependence upon greater than human powers, we would realise human potential at last. Energies set free by knowledge would increase human felicity without limit. By about the middle of the secular age, quite humble people could routinely speak, as they do in Chekhov's comedies, in the following sort of way: 'we will not live to see it, and nor will our children, but a time is coming when human beings will at last be truly happy, and they will look back on our labours and sacrifices with gratitude even as they shake their heads over our quaintly old-fashioned and still superstitious customs and inhibitions'.

By the end of the secular age the prospect had changed. We were getting ever stronger reason to regard the human world as subject to meaningless, convulsive and unpredictable change. The ever-quickening pace of technological alteration was enabling impersonal, corporate entities, relentless pursuers of economic power and wealth, to switch their capital from place to place at will, quickly making redundant not only individuals but historic communities in which the identity of successive generations of individuals had been found. Bereft of another world and ever more imperilled, 'everymensch' – everywoman, everyman – found herself or himself ever more devoid of substance. The sciences were ever more able to look through the individual to the meaningless chemistry beneath. For the doctor, everymensch had become a mere patient, with a life to be prolonged without limit to the extent that funds allowed. For the counsellor, everymensch is a case, to be listened to with a kindly expertise that never answers back, never ventures the kind of personal response to which one might in turn respond in self-discovery. Nor can the future generations to whom Chekhov's characters look forward be counted upon, for what earlier generations would assuredly regard as progress turns out to be taken entirely for granted, without a thought, let alone gratitude, by later generations who are preoccupied with their own novel grievances.

In those countries, such as the Soviet Union, where the secular age expressed itself most vehemently and thoroughly, a generation has come into being of whom it is said that many believe in nothing whatever. It was a disaster, the secular age, now ending.

If I may, as strategists often do, employ the model of rational decision-making – assuming that human beings are rational in order to understand them – then I am surely on strong ground if I suggest that the disasters of the secular age are such that it is reasonable to expect human beings now to reconsider that most characteristic movement of the secular age, its repudiation of the world to come. Ever more benighted in this world, do we not have ever more ground to reconsider whether we should not dwell in imagination and hope upon a new world to redress the balance of the old?

What I am saying connects closely with what is often said about fundamentalist revivals. It is a commonplace that the dislocations of modernisation have encouraged such developments, and that the implications for security are far-reaching. I am saying something of the same thing but I am not saying it in the same way. I am not saying that out there, in the underdeveloped or developing world there are these irrational regressions which constitute a technical and techno-political problem for us in the advanced world. I am saying that times have changed, and that here, in the vanguard of history, time is up for the secular age. Human beings would be crazy to continue to identify themselves primarily in secular terms. A return to the thought that this world is not our home, that we do not and should not hope to belong here, is eminently sensible.

This is of course a frightening thought for the student of security, to whom no commonplace is more familiar than the belief that religious enthusiasm makes any security arrangement far more difficult and unstable. And I do not deny that the age which may be dawning may well be one of terrifying fanaticism, in which we fight over the disagreements into which human beings are so readily drawn whenever they speculate about the life to come, about that larger realm within which, for all we know, the natural world may be contained. But the problem of reckless fanaticism is far from being peculiar to an age of faith. The Third Reich and Stalinism have been characteristic expressions of the secular age, sufficient to make clear that the determination to find fulfilment in this world is far from guaranteeing prudent moderation in either ends or means.

If the 1990s, and beyond, promise or threaten us and our descendants with ever-increasing instability in this world, most notably through the restless immobility of international capital, and if the rational response to this is for human beings to recognise the bankruptcy of secularism and to betake themselves to a passionate retesting of the scope for finding salvation in some larger vision than any that is confined to nature, then profoundly disruptive energies must be expected. But it would be mistaken to regard these as barbarous incursions upon an empire of reason with which we can identify. Rather we should remember that these demonic energies have been as vigorous in the secular age as they have ever been. And we should remember that we are not totally unguided and alone in responding to them.

Throughout the world, profoundly creative cultural resources exist for directing the craving for a greater security than this world can afford in directions that bring with them prudent moderation rather than the heedless aggressiveness of the mere fanatic. The world religions and such religion-like 'philosophies' as Confucianism express in their different ways the common sense that love towards each individual human being, past, present and future has a power and importance that far surpasses everything else in life. In those religions and philosophies that recognise superhuman powers, this love is considered the supreme characteristic of the divine, its paramount claim to be worshipped. In religions and philosophies which do not venture to speak of the superhuman, our lives are located within a normative cosmic order that explains human suffering in terms of the imperfections of our love. In each of these incompatible and frequently warring cultural heritages, the hapless individual is offered an identity beyond the vicissitudes of this world, an ultimate security.

The offer is always conditional, and the rational will embrace it only as a last resort, for it goes against the grain of much that we call human, and demands submission of the self. In the abstract, this is the most frightening feature of all such systems of thought from the political or sociological viewpoint, since it readies the individual to be the unthinking instrument of a vicious higher power. But the world religions and many kindred philosophies have at their centres, not the violent disregard of the individual that typifies the Third Reich and Stalinism, but the promise that each individual is loved.

Whether such promises can be believed depends, humanly speaking, on the kind of shape that the god or supranatural order turns out in practice to have. There is nothing magic about the mere language of sanctity. Nietzsche pointed out that a good war sanctifies any cause, and every religion is fenced about with warnings against false gods. In the secular age, we students of politics and security have been systematically encouraged to abstract from the vastly complicated and difficult problems that arise if we suppose ourselves to be radically and practically committed within the familiar range of religions and philosophies. We have confined our attention to a political order that has a long history of having been painfully constructed in separation from the holy – the state as distinct from the church. The vehement human demand for a stable identity, an ultimate security, has, of course, continued to operate, and its characteristic results have not gone unstudied. But their political designation, for example as nationalism, has been resolutely external.

I am guessing that the secular age is over, and that we are entering a new age of greater directness, in which the quest for identity has to be addressed directly, not least in politics. The time for a strategy of the indirect approach is over. Throughout the secular age, benevolent optimists hoped that the material improvement of human life would bring with it an improvement of morals. This has not happened to anything like the extent that had been hoped, or that we need. Public spirit is very far from being the characteristic mood, let alone the governing principle, in the lives of ordinary people in the most advanced countries. It is true that a television representation of extreme suffering can elicit much sympathy and some cash, but such things are subject to what the professionals call 'compassion fatigue'. We as individuals do not experience the world's justice and peace as basic to our identity. We have to struggle to keep intact the sense that it has anything to do with us as individuals, immersed as we are in a culture that has been consciously guided by the indirect approach.

The secular age has tackled the problem of identity in two main ways. The direct approach has been that which is typified by nationalism. The individual is pressed by all the resources of a formidable state and party apparatus to identify with a higher collective entity, of which he or she is but a part, as a finger or individual hair is part of the body. This can be felt as a solution of the problem only when the nation is intensely active and imposing demands without limit upon its 'members', notably during the enthusiastic phases of war or revolution. As a rational solution to the problem of identity, it is a non-starter. Nations are as mortal as individuals. It is hardly a rational overcoming of, say, grief at the death of a beloved son in a terrorist incident to think of him as a part of a larger whole – the nation – unless it is supposed, absurdly, that the nation is immortal; otherwise, the grief ought rationally to be transferred forward to the time when the nation will disappear. Only by appeal to an order beyond nature, beyond the eleven dimensions in which all things shall pass away, does it make sense to take comfort that the loved one died as part of a larger whole. The direct approach is hopeless.

The indirect approach postulates a lesser order within which things can be done which are hoped to improve matters on the larger scale. For example, we might suppose with the classical economists that a free market can improve the material condition of human life without limit, and hope that this development within the lesser realm of economics will somehow enable the individual to find herself or himself in the larger realm of human life as a whole. I do not deny that improvements of this kind may perhaps be effective within limits. But I do deny that they can in any rational way support the underlying tendency of the secular age, to concentrate exclusively on this world for our identity. It may be that the more leisured and public life which can only come with material conditions far beyond the poor peasant can make it more likely that a person should come to understand that what is really important in human life is love. But all this means is that improved material conditions can perhaps help people to look beyond this world towards one or more of those supernatural beings or powers that are widely believed, despite the secular age, to embody that which is valuable beyond time, and to promise a secure identity.

I have referred to identity at two levels, whose connection we now need to examine. At one level I have suggested that it may become fundamentally important that the great powers find their identity in the public spirit with which they participate in the UN-system. At another level I have urged that if human beings are rational then the widely-expected, ever more rapidly changing economic order, prognosticates a great revival of other-worldly concern, not least in the most advanced nations. I now turn to the relation between these.

A New Identity for a New Age?

One change which we are already witnessing, and which no one expects to be reversed, is that the whole world is becoming ever more rapidly represented to the consciousness of an ever larger number of human beings, especially in the advanced countries. The quality of this representation, the capacity of the media to do more than convey vastly inadequate caricatures, is much debated; but the awareness of the whole globe is indisputable and irresistible. For this dim consciousness to develop into something that is systematically useful, we need a new kind of political order that is inseparably bound up with what I have said about the UN. I am very far from speaking of the kind of new information order (characterised in the UN as a New International Information Order) that would, in effect, empower corrupt governments to control for their own purposes global access to information about their countries. What each one of us needs to be able to know is, where his or her duties lie in contributing to the effective working of that limited oligarchy the United Nations; not just any kind of effectiveness, but the operation of its central organs and special agencies in such a way that we as individuals can find our identity, and can *only* find our identity, through the great powers exercising leadership in pursuit of the UN's proper objectives and, above all, the objective of security.

As an example, let me go back to my reconstructed radical ecologist. I hope to have persuaded her or him, first, that our existing 'philosophy' does not need to be replaced by a new, non-anthropocentric attitude towards nature; and secondly, that the urgent needs for action on pollution and the dolphin should be analysed and formulated in internationalist terms, to find their place in an order which is neither world government nor unlimited sovereignty, but the limited oligarchy of the UN. My discussion of the new age that may be dawning enables me to amplify these earlier suggestions, and to make them more solid. First, I agree with the ecologist that we need something new as regards the moral/spiritual domain to the extent that the old domain is that of the secular age. Indeed, secondly the rapacity with which the last two centuries have ransacked the earth with such disastrous results for the environment has derived no small part of its urgency from the quest for identity. To the extent that our lives are governed by an awareness that this world is not ultimate, we are better equipped to exercise restraint in such matters, from love for our successors (and the dolphin).

Thirdly the revival of preoccupation with identity offers to such as the radical ecologist a framework which is much more inclusive and stable than any that could derive from the pressure-group political culture of pure ecology. If that love which many call divine is to be the guiding principle in the lives of populations who are ever more aware, as we are, of the desperate need to govern our planet as a whole, then the consequent practical concerns are intrinsically those of politics and public administration rather than sectarian.

Thus I am imagining that it may become increasingly possible to speak to public-spirited people with a great variety of concerns in the following sort of way, not as an abstract and practically meaningless set of platitudes but with the force and substance of a kind of internationalism that is neither world government nor unbridled sovereignty but the beneficent limited oligarchy of the great powers. One might be able to say, 'Your particular concerns should rationally be analysed and presented, as they will be assessed, in terms of a certain kind of global system. The largest responsibilities in this system devolve upon the great powers, which have the largest scope to bear such a burden. This is not an oppressive doctrine, for the world is divided into states whose citizens have outgrown the secular age and whose spiritual development has been in the direction of striving by every means to make the love which some call divine into the guiding principle of their individual and collective lives; and who therefore attach central importance to the moral quality of leadership as provided by the great powers. This spiritual maturity has developed, and is continuing to develop, through the loving, forthright, mutual exploration of adherents of the many religious and philosophical traditions. As they try to explain themselves to one another, and to understand themselves in the light of this discourse, the adherents of these traditions do not eliminate all disagreements by any means, but they find it increasingly impossible to believe that their disagreements are of kinds that can find rational expression in persecution or war. The quiet pursuit of a shared understanding of salvation lends weight to the civic demand for a reputable politics.'

We have been concerned with security in the 1990s and beyond. I have expressed this in terms that connect military security with speculation about the nature of our insecurity as individuals. Hobbes would not find my material surprising, though he and many a political theorist after him would sneer at my handling of this material. He considers the spiritual to be inherently irrational and divisive, the most potent of all sources of disorder and war. He is a frank materialist, and the urgent desire for a security beyond the little world of nature is entirely excluded from his thought. He begins *Leviathan* by inviting the reader to engage in introspection: 'He that is to govern a whole Nation, must read in himself, not this or that particular man; but Man-kind . . . when I shall have set down my own reading orderly, and perspicuously, the pains left another, will be only to consider, if he also find not the same in himself, For this kind of Doctrine, admitteth no other Demonstration'.[2]

In Hobbes we find a wonderfully pungent exposition of unbridled sovereignty. Many who oppose the spirit of Hobbes are driven to argue in terms of world government. I have tried to suggest that a new age may be dawning in which, if we look within, we may find a configuration quite different from that discerned by Hobbes; and this because he, great precursor of the secular age, systematically disregards that desire for ultimate security which cannot be satisfied within the natural world.

3

Madness Under Fire

Brian Bond

Professional historians are primarily concerned to understand and bring to life the past in its own terms rather than to ransack history in search of lessons relevant to the present age. Though others may claim to derive lessons from their work, historians who go looking for them are likely to pay a high price in terms of a loss of objectivity. Nevertheless, in the discipline of military history the didactic tradition was enormously powerful and continued to be influential until very recently.

Professor John Gooch, for example, has described such distinguished military writers as Major-General J.F.C. Fuller and Sir Basil Liddell Hart as 'plunderers' and 'raiders' who 'used history to do little more than authenticate strategic propositions'. Even today modern military historians, more than specialists in other branches of strategic studies, may feel under pressure to do research and reach conclusions which are regarded as 'relevant' to current defence problems. This is particularly the case with military historians who work closely with the armed services, since the latter are understandably in search of a usable and useful past and only rarely value historical scholarship for its own sake.

Irritating though the pressure for contemporary relevance may sometimes be, military historians who prefer to seek refuge in the archives, and to publish only in learned journals, simply abandon the field to others with less knowledge – or fewer scruples. Historical notions, generalisations and myths are frequently invoked in contemporary debate or used to underpin assumptions when comparisons and contrasts are made with supposedly similar episodes in the past. The 1930s were very much in vogue in the light of the Iraqi aggression against Kuwait in August 1990, with frequent references to the 'spirit of Munich', which is usually taken to demonstrate the folly of trying to appease aggressors in a vain effort to avoid war: thus the heading 'Lords reminded of 1930s lesson in shrinking from war'.[1] Let us, therefore, explore this analogy a little further to test its applicability to recent and present international conflicts.

The appeasement policy of the Western allies involved in 'the spirit

36

of Munich' revolved around the fate of the Sudetenland area in pre-war Czechoslovakia, several hundred miles away. Even more than the Sudetenland, however, the Falkland Islands were a very 'far away country' about which the British public knew little before April 1982. But, like the Sudeten issue, the Falklands were a direct British responsibility; a flagrant act of aggression had occurred; the enemy was in 'our league'; and a military operation to recover the islands was (just about) feasible, given United Nations' approval and tacit United States' support. Military victory was comparatively inexpensive in lives lost, secured its immediate goal and led to the additional bonus of the overthrow of the Argentinian junta. In August 1990 Kuwait was also 'far away' and 'little known' in Chamberlain's terms; few of us could have drawn it accurately in a sketch map before the Iraqi invasion, but we are all Middle Eastern strategists now, in the light of a war conducted in the glare of instant news analysis.

During the amazingly rapid and far-reaching transformation of eastern Europe culminating in the unexpected reunification of Germany, which was predicted by few pundits indeed, there was a period which seemed eerily like a replay of 1939, with ethnic Germans in southern Poland clamouring for inclusion in the new Reich and Chancellor Kohl refusing initially to confirm the Oder-Neisse frontier and then agreeing to sign a piece of paper. The Poles were reported to be so alarmed that they were asking Soviet commanders in the Red Army garrison in Poland not to evacuate their territory. Poor Mr Nicholas Ridley terminated his political career by some tactless remarks regarding Germany's likely dominance in the future Europe, when it seemed clear to most observers that a united Germany's dominance would be based on economic rather than military power. At least in 1990 the Poles were spared the kiss of death of an Anglo-French guarantee.

The exploits of Saddam Hussein have elicited many comparisons with Hitler. In the initial reaction to the invasion of Kuwait the strong preference of the United Nations and most of its members was for economic sanctions as an alternative to armed force. In this respect a more appropriate comparison can be made with Mussolini and the Abyssinian crisis of 1935/36 rather than with Hitler and the 'spirit of Munich'. In the Abyssinian case, Britain and France, as the two most effective instruments of the League of Nations, did not see eye to eye. Sanctions were applied only half-heartedly and Mussolini, to all intents and purposes, secured his conquest.

In the debates over sanctions in 1990 moral fervour – and the laudable hope of avoiding an air and ground war – seemed to push aside any investigation of the historical effectiveness of sanctions – though their failure to work over Rhodesia from 1965 to 1979 provided a recent memory of some relevance. Had economic sanctions without the accompanying use of force ever caused a considerable power to change its policy to the extent, for example, of withdrawing from occupied territory? Blockade by land and sea have often occurred in war but less often as an alternative to war. Vulnerable though Iraq was to a range of economic sanctions, particularly given its dependence on oil exports, the prospects of success in securing withdrawal from Kuwait were never good, given the probable time required for them to bite sufficiently and the potential fragility of the anti-Iraq coalition.

During the First World War the allied naval blockade eventually caused suffering and even starvation to the poorer sections of society in Germany in 1918/19; but is that what the supporters of economic sanctions wanted in Iraq? Alternatively, in the case of Japan in 1941, the United States' imposition of an oil embargo was the trigger for Japan's all-out attack against American and European possessions in the Pacific. This was hardly what the supporters of sanctions in 1990 wanted in the Middle East. The sanctions policy of the UN coalition against Iraq, for as long as it lasted, provides another case study in the circumstances in which economic sanctions might achieve desired political objectives. There will almost certainly be more calls for sanctions as the UN takes on greater responsibilities for international disorder. Perhaps now the historical experience of economic sanctions will receive the careful scrutiny it should have been given before.

As for the resemblances between Saddam Hussein and Hitler, they grew more depressingly convincing with every passing day of the Gulf War and its aftermath. Both represent megalomaniacs who seized power at the second attempt after one failed coup; both fostered a cult of their own personality; relied largely on their own cunning and willpower, had no trusted advisers on whom to rely for objective information, let alone a responsible cabinet, council or democratic parliament. Neither had an extensive knowledge of the outside world and both were able to utilise a near-total control of the media. Both encouraged a fanatical ideology – Nazism and the Ba'ath party's unrealistic bid to unite the Arab world. Both, it must now be grimly admitted, actually welcomed war, thereby completely thwarting the good intentions of their opponents to avoid conflict by an appeal to reason. Saddam Hussein displayed alarming 'Hitler symptoms' in what has become generally known as a bunker mentality; refusing to admit defeat and/or being prepared to sacrifice his own country and people.

However, when one turns from the personalities involved in a conflict to the larger political issues, the differences between the Munich era and the recent Gulf conflict are more striking than the similarities. Hitler's political programme, however barbaric within Germany, seemed more legitimate than Saddam Hussein's enterprise, at least until Hitler's seizure of Prague in March 1939; namely the recovery or absorption of German-speaking peoples into the Reich. Saddam's occupation of Kuwait, where there was no pro-Iraq party and only the most tenuous political claims to disputed borders, more closely resembled the German invasion of Poland.

In 1938 Germany was believed to be more capable of hurting its main Western opponents (Britain and France) through strategic bombing than they were of hurting Germany. This was not the case with Iraq, though one wonders if the United Nations powers would have been so willing to confront Iraq had it been a fully developed nuclear power. Organised international opposition to Hitler was virtually non-existent in 1939; even in France and Britain appeasement did not disappear with the outbreak of war and in both countries a minority regarded the Soviet Union as the real enemy. By contrast, though in terms of its government and political culture Kuwait was hardly a more deserving cause for rescue by force than Poland (and much less than Belgium in 1914), in the curious international circumstances of 1990 a unique consensus was reached in the United Nations that Iraqi aggression must be stopped. It was a somewhat precarious consensus, but it was maintained for sufficient time to allow the coalition powers to achieve a swift and devastating military victory over Iraqi forces.

Perhaps the most obvious and important contrast between Munich and the Gulf crisis is that neither the Soviet Union nor the United States was involved in 1939, the latter from choice and the former through deliberate exclusion from the Munich conference by Britain and France. It is doubtful whether Hitler would have risked a general European war if either, let alone both, had been formally ranged against him. In the Gulf crisis the United States played the dominant role throughout, while the Soviet Union's formal support was essential to the imposition of sanctions and, albeit negatively, in the conduct of the war.

In 1938/39 Britain and France were inhibited in resisting Germany by a perception of military inferiority on land and in the air, linked with a fear that war could not be kept limited and, in particular, that Italy and Japan would take advantage of Germany's initial successes to start a world war. This partly explains, though it does not justify, the sacrifice of Czechoslovakia and the Anglo-French willingness to put pressure on Poland to make further concessions in order to avoid a general war.

Chamberlain and his supporters were at least correct in their assumption that a long and total war would be disastrous for Britain even if it emerged on the winning side. In the Gulf crisis, however, the assumption was that Iraq, faced with overwhelming odds, could be defeated quickly without the war spreading, though Saddam Hussein's attempts to draw Israel into the conflict with *Scud* missile attacks against Israeli territory tested this assumption severely. In the event, it proved to be correct, though if the war had not been won quickly a different result would certainly have been possible.

These necessarily brief and sketchy comparisons with the Munich era demonstrate the truth of the fact that history does not repeat itself, that knowledge of the past does not equip scholars to predict what will happen in the future, and that too close an identification of a contemporary leader with a past dictator (as Eden notoriously did in the Suez crisis in 1956, seeing Gamel Abdul Nasser as a new manifestation of Hitler) can be disastrous. It remains to be seen whether the personal similarities between Saddam and Hitler will persist to the bitter end in self-destruction in a ruined country.

As commentators on contemporary affairs, such as Edward Luttwak[2] are already pointing out, there are numerous inconsistencies, flaws and paradoxes in the United States' and the United Nations' behaviour before and during the Gulf crisis; for example, the West and the Soviet Union have supplied Middle East dictatorships and sheikhdoms with modern weapons on a vast scale; Kuwait and the Gulf States are anything but liberal democracies; and the overthrow of Saddam Hussein is no guarantee of improved security either within Iraq or between it and its neighbours.

Nevertheless, and however patchy the record of the United Nations since 1945 in resisting aggression, it seems clear that having made such a tremendous commitment to defeating Saddam Hussein, the nations involved in the Gulf War coalition (and the United States in particular) could not afford to fail in the primary aim of ejecting Iraqi forces from Kuwait, without a disastrous loss of prestige and self-confidence. Whether such national and international consensus and cohesion can be maintained in the longer term into what is referred to as the 'new world order' must be doubtful.

Historians must be both impressed and disturbed by the astonishing development of communications (and especially television) in influencing issues of war and peace in open societies. Impressed, because it is absolutely necessary and salutary that on every occasion a large majority of the electorate must be convinced in open debate that the resort to war is just and is not the worst evil that can occur. Disturbing, because it is extremely difficult to give due weight to complex political and strategic factors as against the powerfully emotive ones of suffering, death and destruction, particularly in conflicts where the enemy's media are ruthlessly controlled by the state.

Although it may take several years for historians to present a rounded and properly documented account of the Gulf War of 1990–1, 'instant' biographies of Saddam Hussein and acounts of the War are already available. In the longer term, historians will expose errors, false assumptions and unforeseen, long-term, costs – or costs that were foreseen and not presented to the public at the time; but they should still be, in principle, sympathetic to those individuals who had to take the awful decision to resort to war.

In the present century war has largely ceased to be an effective 'instrument of policy' for the aggressor, but it remains a valid and – sometimes – effective resort for nations who are prepared to defend themselves and others.

4

Politics as Government and Politics as Security

Michael Clarke

The relationship between politics and international security is self-evidently close. 'Security' is a perceptual commodity that cannot be deduced and is thus an intrinsically political calculation; and 'politics' must necessarily be about those arrangements which prevent mankind from slipping into the insecurities associated with a state of nature, or a state of anarchy, which all but anarchists have defined as undesirable. Yet if the concepts 'security' and 'politics' appear to be logically inseparable, it does not follow that the disciplines supporting them will be so too. In fact, one of the surprises that greets anyone studying the discipline of politics, is how cursory is the overlap between the organisation of each subject area: the differences seem to outweigh the similarities. In order to offer a political science perspective on the future of security after the cold war it is first necessary to examine the somewhat curious relationship between politics and the study of international security. In this respect, there is also a distinction between the study and the substance of these subjects.

The Study of Politics and International Security

Let us establish at the outset that politics is the core discipline in which we are interested. It is a central subject in the humanities and is the grandparent of international politics, political philosophy, public administration, the study of democracy, and so on. These are all sub-disciplines of politics. But there is a confusion in the popular debate about this, since when modern students talk about 'politics' they normally mean the study of domestic political processes, or else comparisons between domestic societies. The grandparent discipline of politics has witnessed an understandable, but increasingly insupportable, dichotomy throughout the twentieth century between politics (understood in this modern sense) and international relations.

42

This dichotomy has been driven mainly by differing assumptions about the nature of security.[1] It has also been driven by the institutions that have supported these two branches of the politics discipline. It is natural, if not always appropriate, that academic institutions and departments established specifically to study particular sub-disciplines should insist on establishing the unique characteristics of their subject and to resent suggestions that perhaps it could be studied just as well somewhere else.

The dichotomy is most clearly illustrated by a comparison of the assumptions underlying comparative politics and international politics. Both are sub-disciplines of politics in the strict, 'grandparent' sense described above. Comparative politics is a key sub-discipline because it represents the attempt to compare and classify political systems in an Aristotelian manner, and is therefore on the conceptual frontier of politics, seeking to develop theories about the very nature of political activity; and international politics because it has been regarded – by definition – as that branch of politics which is concerned with the problem of insecurity at the inter-state level.[2] The differences between the assumptions that both sub-disciplines have adopted were very marked. Comparative politics was concerned with order and legitimacy. Its classical exponents, Aristotle and John Stuart Mill, no less than those of the early twentieth century, such as James Bryce or Woodrow Wilson, were concerned precisely to investige those political circumstances that created the order and legitimacy characteristic of an ideal state. International politics, on the other hand, was created as an explicit sub-discipline in the twentieth century precisely because of the apparent collapse of order and legitimacy occasioned by the First World War. It was felt necessary to study more carefully the disorder of international affairs and investigate more closely whether international politics could be domesticated to make it more like the ordered politics that was assumed to exist within the state. Comparative politics was therefore concerned with political institutions: devices to encapsulate legitimacy and to promote constructive values within society. International politics, on the other hand, was concerned less with institutions than with diplomacy. International institutions to promote similar values to those of domestic society were desired by many of the early writers in the field; but there could be no gainsaying the fact that, unless or until such institutions existed, diplomacy was the only alternative method through which to promote even a minimum degree of order, let alone constructive values. Similarly, comparative politics was concerned with divisions of labour within domestic society. Divisions of labour are both inevitable and natural in any society and their political implications are one of the driving forces behind all domestic politics. International politics, on the other hand, was based on an assumption that all the members of its society – individual sovereign states – were driven by the imperative of self-sufficiency: all had to be capable of defending, feeding, and organising themselves by a mixture of physical capability (such as military forces) and diplomatic action (such as alliances and agreements). Divisions of labour could exist in international society, but if so, they were assumed to be matters of convenience; there was nothing natural or inevitable about them.

Finally, the philosophical underpinnings of each subject – derived from the same tradition of political philosophy that grew from Plato and Aristotle, through St Augustine and Thomas Aquinas and then Machiavelli to the 'moderns' of Hobbes, Locke and Hegel – tended to diverge somewhat in the twentieth century as the differences between states and people were considered more carefully. In the philosophy that backed up the discipline of politics, the critical relationships were between man and man, whereas in the philosophy that informed international politics, the equivalent was the relationship between one state and another. But as modern writers such as Hedley Bull, Herbert Butterfield, Martin Wight and Kenneth Waltz have pointed out in many distinguished works, a society of states was somewhat different from a society of people. People tend towards the average in their physical and intellectual capacities, whereas states tend towards the extremes of size, strength and abilities; people are physically vulnerable to an extent that states are evidently not (few states have genuinely died in the last 500 years); people can be assumed to be unitary political actors since there can be no smaller political entity than a single person, whereas individual states may be far from unitary actors as their constituent parts pursue their own particular interests. Not least, states do not in themselves embody human motivations; they are abstractions which cannot feel hunger, humiliation, sleeplessness or gratitude. The health of a state is quite different from the well-being of its leaders, still less of its citizens. Some of these insights yield conclusions which may appear perverse. States are much less physically vulnerable than people, and yet live in an environment in which the fight for survival is never far from the surface. States have vastly differing natural capacities, yet do not engage in extensive divisions of labour, and so on. Nevertheless, it was a reasonable assumption for twentieth century writers to make that, if states were self-evidently not people, then conditions in the society between them would be vastly different from those existing within a society of people.

Such differing assumptions tended to be reinforced by the way in which both sub-disciplines evolved. The twentieth century discipline of politics developed from older studies of 'government', 'law' and more recently, 'public administration'; while international politics developed after 1919 precisely in response to a perceived breakdown in the application of government, law and effective public administration at the international level. It suited both sub-disciplines, therefore, to go their separate ways. Comparative politics needed a clear boundary to delineate its territory and establish which laws and institutions were relevant to its concerns. The nation-state provided such a boundary. Inside it there existed 'government' which might be democratic or totalitarian, traditional or modern, efficient or otherwise; outside it there was, well, if not quite 'anarchy' then certainly something different in kind.

International politics, on the other hand, needed an identity. It developed this within its first 20 years in the notion of realism: a paradigm of world politics in which the state was the basic unit and the relations between states were dominated by the management of power politics between them. If power was managed efficiently, then there could be a form of diplomatic order and other political refinements could thereby exist in the world; if badly, then nothing else would prevent the outbreak of violence and disorder. Realism, therefore, provided international politics with an identity that, as it happened, was entirely consistent with the boundary that comparative politics sought to define.

The boundary is to some extent legitimate, but it was always overstated and the conditions of contemporary world politics, no less than in the domestic arena, render it increasingly dubious. It was overstated because it assumed too much consistency in the defining unit – the nation state. The population of states in the world grew from just over 50 in 1945 to almost 170 by the end of the 1980s and is set to reach perhaps the 200 mark in the foreseeable future. As the number of states has increased so has the diversity between them. They all have a common legal status; but this comes to mean less and less when comparing, for example, one of the older European states that grew out of the struggles for nationhood of the sixteenth century with one of the African states declared independent in the mid-1960s, which has had statehood, in effect, thrust upon it and must now define a 'nation' after being recognised as a state. The institution of the state, in other words, should not be regarded as defining with great consistency the content of political relationships that will exist between them. The relationship between, say, the government and society of the United States and that of Costa Rica, still less of Panama, bears little relationship to that between, say, the USA and Germany, or the USA and Japan. The more states that exist in the world, the less they have constituted the defining characteristic of an international political system.

Apart from being overstated, the boundary between domestic and international politics has also been undermined by the conditions of modern world politics. The growth in world communications and transport, in increasingly global modes of production, in the ease of international investment, and so on, have changed the picture some-what. It is not that these trends have necessarily diminished the political power of the state in any given case – though there is a vigorous debate over this point – but rather that they have led to the growth of other political institutions and processes which have come to share the international political arena with the state to a greater extent than ever before. Domestic and international politics have – in effect – all been rendered part of the same political arena by a number of developments. The multinationalisation of most big busi-nesses (more powerful an influence than the growth of multinational companies in the 1950s and 1960s), and the international politics that exists between major firms around the world, is obviously one. So too is the appearance of so many international functional insti-tutions to control air traffic, regulate trade, monetary movements, data transmission, and broadcasting, as is the development of some fairly powerful international regimes, such as those of the European Community's agricultural or competition policy, or of the inter-national oil market. There are many examples. Whether or not the later twentieth century has undermined the power of the state as an institution, there can be little doubt that it has reduced its conceptual usefulness as a boundary between comparative politics and inter-national politics.

Strategic Studies

Strategic studies, as a branch of international politics, has both enjoyed the benefits of the somewhat artificial dichotomy between domestic and international politics and suffered the consequences as it has come under savage scrutiny in recent years. Strategic studies grew up in the early 1950s, drawing inspiration from a long tradition of military historians and analysts and a number of impressive strategic theorists of the early twentieth century. Though its origins could be traced some way back, there can be little doubt that the circumstances of the cold war and the advent of the nuclear age provided a powerful impetus to the growth of strategic studies. The subject embodied international political realism in a rather dramatic way, and the bipolarity of the cold war provided an application for it that was both intellectually precise and politically relevant. For a subject that was still seeking a proper identity, strategic studies provided an example of what international political realism could achieve: a number of respectable theories of conflict and conflict-prevention, and a central theory – namely deterrence – which provided apparently testable hypotheses that were pertinent to policy-makers.[3] Thus leading American strategists of the 1950s went into government and gave tangible political expression to their theories of what was stabilising or destabilising for nuclear deterrence, how the use of force could be graduated to achieve particular political objectives and how crises could be efficiently and peacefully managed.

For some, this indicated that international politics had finally grown up. Realism had been vindicated by the bitter experiences of the 1930s and there was now no serious dispute that states were the principal units of world politics, between whom peace could only be kept through the exercise of armed diplomacy. The living embodiments of realism were conflict and deterrence theories. These were genuinely elegant; they were parsimonious, capable – as Michael Nicholson has shown[4] – of mathematical calculation, and they could be used both to test and to generate hypotheses. Most of all, the application of realist thinking seemed to have matured because strategic studies appeared to have the virtue of being systemic. The theories of conflict and deterrence that were articulated were assumed to be applicable throughout the system of post-war world politics: deterrence logic was thought to work in a general as well as a specific sense. Nuclear capability automatically conferred a deterrent logic on the relationship between one nuclear armed state and another. Similarly, graduated conflict theories, counter-insurgency techniques or crisis management was assumed to have some general applicability throughout the international system, notwithstanding the fact that there were bound to be varying conditions in which they would be applied. Strategic studies thus reinforced the principles of its underlying realism, for in being systemic it assumed that the states which were the units of the system behaved in a sufficiently similar way to attribute some common patterns to the system as a whole. And since the theories of strategic studies became so linked to the practice of them, certainly within the United States government, they gave all the appearances of being inescapable facts of life; indeed almost scientific facts.

This, however, proved to be a misleading confidence, prompted largely by the glamour that the cold war bestowed on a subject apparently so central to its functioning. Strategic studies was not as systemic as first appeared, or if it was, then only at a superficial level. Good strategists, like good realist thinkers, always acknowledged the dangers of according too much systemic virtue to their subject.[5] They explicitly acknowledged that the central conflict between the two superpowers was both historically and geographically untypical and have been reluctant to claim any general applicability for the dynamics of the conflict that they observed. The problem was that, in a critical earlier period during the 1950s and early 1960s, there were not enough 'good' strategists around. The subject slipped too easily into an implicit acceptance that what appeared to hold for the superpowers would hold for any powers. This was never more true than in the most eloquent expression of strategic studies: the concept of deterrence.

Deterrence theory was clearly articulated and developed by a generation of, chiefly, American strategists who knew very little about the Soviet Union. The most important fact about the Soviet Union was assumed to be that it was a giant power in possession of nuclear weapons, not that it was Soviet, or predominently Russian, or a continental land power that had fought a bitter war, or even that it was Communist. It was assumed to be an intellectual and military counterpart to the United States, and no matter how much the Soviets protested that they did not believe in deterrence theory, it was maintained that they could hardly ignore it and – since their adversary *did* believe in deterrence – could not avoid it anyway. Interestingly, the Soviet Union seems to have been highly ambiguous about deterrence: at an official level leaders really did not believe in it, and yet seemed to become somewhat clumsy practitioners of it at both the tactical and the strategic force level during the early 1970s.

Strategists therefore worked out the subtleties of a nuclear deterrent relationship, and in particular, the conditions for a stable deterrent relationship, which was firmly rooted in the relations between the United States and the Soviet Union, but which was felt also to exist in an 'existential' sense. That is to say, whether or not states choose to play the deterrence game, the rules of it will nevertheless tend to operate in all cases where nuclear weapons are known, or even believed, to exist: existential deterrence, it is assumed, is a fact of life wherever the capability for effective strategic retaliation is present.

The conditions in which stable deterrence was felt to exist, however, drew heavily upon a context that was peculiar to the cold war. It assumed that only two actors were involved in the relationship. It is difficult to see how deterrence can remain stable where multiple actors, perhaps of varying capabilities, are involved. It assumed that the actors were in full control of their forces and of their decision-making capabilities. States would be able to act purposefully and their behaviour would reflect, fairly precisely, their intentions. It assumed that states acted rationally; that is, that they would have a similar perception of their own best interests and would regard the initiation of a nuclear exchange as a catastrophe to be avoided. And it assumed that weapons were only developed because of a perceived deterrent need for them: developments in deterrence theory could not be driven by the innovations of new weapons systems.

Not surprisingly, such assumptions seemed to be questionable not only because of developments between the superpowers but also by the broader trends of world politics during the 1970s. The several tasks that nuclear deterrence was called upon to perform came to seem infinitely more complicated, whilst new and elaborate weapons systems became more generally available for the delivery of nuclear weapons. The concept of deterrence was thus invoked to justify increasingly tortured defence-policy arguments – for more tactical weapons to 'couple' the USA with others, for devices to 'extend' deterrence, for space-based defensive systems, and for nuclear war-fighting options – which stretched the concept so thinly that it seriously diminished its specific meaning. Any new strategic doctrine or weapon system that could be used in a war came to be a component of deterrence – a further proof of one's willingness to use military force – and it became difficult to think of any military innovation that could not be claimed to be necessary on the grounds of maintaining the credibility of deterrence.

In short, the mainstream of strategic studies ran itself into a corner of its own making. By the late 1970s it seemed to have become a micro subject, concerned primarily with new weapons systems and some quite 'theological' debates on the refinements of deterrence. It was divorced from the macro political realities of a world that was no longer defined by the cold war. And it came in for a good deal of criticism that was at once justified and yet which also risked throwing out the baby with the bathwater. Strategic studies had been beguiled by the intricacies of deterrence theory, and while it had not entirely neglected other dimensions of the subject – such as the study of arms control, civil-military relations, weapons proliferation, arms technology transfer, the trends in non-nuclear weaponry, and the institutions of security around the world – it either paid them scant attention or else cast them primarily in the light of deterrence theory.

Throughout this time – the 40 years since the beginning of the cold war – students of domestic politics had made little or no impact on strategic studies, though there was a great deal they might have offered which could have helped to prevent its slide into an exclusive micro-study of conflict. They could have challenged the somewhat simple assumptions upon which deterrence theory was based – assumptions of political control over key decisions, over technological development, the assumption of rational behaviour, and so on – and helped to keep strategic studies firmly grounded. Or again, the sub-discipline of policy analysis began to make great strides during the 1950s and 1960s in understanding the imperfections and diverse forces that drove along health policy, industrial policy, or macro-economic policy in the major Western democracies, but very little of that effort was applied to the study of defence policies, still less to strategic planning. The work upon which Graham Allison established his reputation in 1969 drew heavily from the early exponents of policy analysis, but the fact that his *Essence of Decision* stood for so long as a (somewhat overrated) milestone in the study of strategic decision-making, only demonstrates how little there was to set against it.

Not until the 1980s, and mainly in the United States – with its influence over world politics apparently in steep decline – did domestic political analysts begin to dissect American defence policy in some detail to reveal more clearly the complex and differing influences that drove it along. And only in the 1980s, in the light of the strategic failures in Vietnam, in the Middle East and around the Third World, was there any significant contribution from other political analysts to challenge the predominently geopolitical assumptions that were characteristic of American strategic planning. Only then was there a significant debate over how well American strategic planners, bolstered by strategic studies, understood the indigenous causes of the conflicts in which the United States became involved. Previous debates on such issues had been marginal: restricted to the anti-Vietnam left, who later also took on American policy in Central and Latin America. But while that debate was sometimes very vigorous, it did not become mainstream. The intellectual left in the United States has always been numerically small, and it was only in the light of manifest and persistent policy failures that their arguments were taken up within the essentially conservative mainstream of American political and intellectual debate.

Even within their own terms of reference, the study of comparative politics and those sub-disciplines of politics that were concerned with domestic society, was surprisingly narrow in focus during the 40 years after 1945 when the world was changing so rapidly. Comparative politics gave little attention to the growth of the Third World and the greater variety of political processes that were emerging among these two-thirds of the world's states which contained over three-quarters of its total population. The subject drew most of its inspiration from the 20 or so pluralist democracies of the Western world and from a somewhat curious abstraction called 'the Communist state'. It was never clear quite where in the world this latter state was to be found, what nationality were its people, nor what language they spoke. But 'the Communist state' was a useful abstraction that helped to point up the contrasts with the democratic pluralism of the West.

This is not to say that analysts of the Communist world were not fully aware of the diversity of those states characterised by one-party Marxist governments. Analysts of the Soviet Union and eastern Europe, still more of Cuba, Angola, China or Vietnam, were only too conscious of the different conditions in which Marxist philosophy was being applied. But comparative politics scholars did not try to integrate knowledge of such diversities into an expanding frame of reference. Since Marxism claimed to be a systemic and consistent approach to government, analysts of comparative politics tended to take that at face value and simply used the abstraction of 'the Communist state' as an agreed point on the spectrum along which types of government were to be classified and judged.

In this respect, the Marxist analysis of politics casts an interesting light on the dichotomy between comparative politics and international security. For Marxism offers an explanation of politics – politics in its guise as the central discipline – which is genuinely systemic and which explicitly bridges the gap between domestic politics and international security. For the Marxist, international politics are only a reflection of the dialectical process wherein social relations within states are working towards their inevitable conclusions. Since the state is ultimately only an instrument of class rule, it will change as class rule comes to an end. And when the state withers away, the society of states will also, presumably, do the same. Modern Marxists have not always seen the process of the withering of the state as being so simple or inevitable, but have nevertheless looked towards a situation in which a new sort of state might exist, wherein different functions of national identification would be performed and only non-antagonistic differences and contradictions would exist between one state and another. A society of states might still exist, but it would be on the basis of a quite different process of politics to anything we have experienced so far. In reducing politics to a fundamental assumption about the relationships between people (i.e., that one will seek to exploit another) and in reducing history to an equally fundamental assumption that it moves in a dialectal, and not a simply random fashion, Marxism provides a magnificent theory of politics that offers explanations and hypotheses for everything that happens in both the domestic and the international political world. To acknowledge its achievement, of course, is not to adopt it as a truth. Whether one regards its basic premises on the nature of politics and history as fundamentals of human existence or oversimplifications of reality, seems to be a matter of taste. More immediately, the explanations and hypotheses about the nineteenth and the twentieth century world that Marxism has offered us have either had to be constantly revised to take account of unanticipated trends, or else have had to be stated at such a high level of abstraction that they tell us very little about the world in which we are interested. This does not necessarily invalidate Marxism. As a method of analysis it is as useful now as it ever was, and as a grand theory of history it cannot – by definition – be disproved. But, as it seems to illuminate less and less about an increasingly complex world, its attractions as a systemic theory have worn somewhat thin. Perhaps we should be content to regard it as *a* theory rather than *the* theory of politics, though to a loyal Marxist, this is a typically pluralist assertion that contradicts the essence of what Marx was trying to do.

So we are left in a quandary. The world around us appears to be going through a series of sea-changes, not merely with the end of the cold war and the breaking up of the Soviet Union, but also with the rapid development of new economic and social processes – the communications revolution, the globalisation of production and so on – that have both integrative and disintegrative effects. The world of the twenty-first century is likely to be characterised by greater political diversity in some respects (such as more states and sub-groups within states) and yet greater integration in others (such as fewer, highly international manufacturing companies). Security challenges in the post-cold war world are also changing rapidly. Yet academics are struggling to keep up with the momentum. The study of international security, and particularly strategic studies, must reorientate itself to new problems and put deterrence back where it belongs as something less than a central, organising device of the subject. And the study of comparative politics and various domestic political processes is faced with the task of crossing the boundaries of the state to consider more carefully the interaction of domestic and international forces. Marxist explanations, as an alternative, seem not worth the effort given the generality of the explanations they offer.

The Substance of Politics and International Security

For our purposes, the question resulting from the analysis above may be stated quite simply: what are the various subdisciplines of politics now able to offer the particular subdiscipline of international politics and, in particular, the study of international security? The contemporary world scene suggests that there are a great many possibilities from which to choose.

International security in the future will have to be set in the context of the high levels of interdependence in the world. This has been evident in all Middle Eastern conflicts since 1956, where war has affected the international oil market. It has become even more marked since 1973, since when shifting balances of power in the region have had an effect on world finance and petrodollars have come to play such an important role in Western financial institutions. It was certainly the case in the Vietnam War, where the Western world as a whole paid a price for the financing of an expensive conflict, not through extra taxation but from American current expenditure and international borrowing. The Gulf War provides an excellent example of the highly interdependent nature of major world conflicts in the later twentieth century: economics, domestic politics, and diplomacy – both of the international coalition and as regards the military operations against Iraq – were locked in a political mesh that directly affected almost 40 countries, the whole of the oil industry, major international institutions, domestic security in some 20 Western states, and which was felt to have a direct bearing on world financial stability. For the coming decade, civil conflicts within the new Europe will almost certainly create problems caused by high levels of interdependence across the continent. A unified Germany brings many territorial and ethnic problems to the very doorstep of the European Community. However Germany and its Community partners react to such conflicts, there can be little doubt that it will be impossible to divorce those reactions from calculations of their domestic economic costs, the costs to European and other companies, their effect on national and regional elections, and their impact on a number of institutions, from the Community itself or NATO to the operations of central banks trying to stabilise volatile currencies.

In short, it is important that we understand the phenomenon of international interdependence in the modern world, for it is likely to be a major dimension in future conflicts; indeed, if we take seriously the prospects of crises in the environment and struggles over water resources and so forth, it may even be a cause of them. The student of domestic politics and the political economist have a great deal to offer here. For the concept of interdependence was well outlined almost 20 years ago in two seminal works by Robert Keohane and Joseph Nye.[6] Since then it has become an accepted term in political debate, but after two decades of general use, the concept of interdependence is still little more than a metaphor that describes an extraordinarily complex political phenomenon. Analysts of international relations have not been able to understand this phenomenon much better over the last two decades, and analysts of strategic studies, still obsessed with deterrence and American ways of thinking geopolitically, have scarcely tried. The essence of interdependence is that it describes connections between actors that are costly for both or all of them to break, such that there is a significant disincentive to do so. Some connections – trade, aid, diplomatic links, sharing of data, membership of institutions – are therefore more interdependent than others. A number could be broken without much cost to some of the parties, others would involve a prohibitive cost to almost all of them. The calculation of the costs of breaking linkages is thus a complex one, since it is highly perceptual and will often be affected by fundamental political reactions.

This is precisely where the analysts of domestic politics and economics are needed. Whether or not interdependence ever achieves the status of an accepted theory (that is, being capable of generating and/or testing worthwhile hypotheses) it is virtually certain that students of conflict in the future will require the relevant data and the insights gained from political studies to understand better the calculus of the interdependent relationships that will surround both future conflicts and the strategic planning which tries to take account of them. A calculation of relevant costs to a state (or any other type of actor for that matter) requires an understanding of the policy-making process that will try to make the relevant calculations, the special domestic interests that will be most affected by a collapse of certain linkages, and the domestic trade-offs that would be occasioned by a breakdown. Conversely, it will also be important to understand the incentives to engage – consciously or not – in linkages that are interdependent by their very nature; and to understand better the ways in which those incentives are felt within domestic society.

We appear to be moving into an era in which economic dimensions loom increasingly large in security issues. There is a great deal of work to be done over the coming years in order to understand this phenomenon properly. It is not too much of a simplification to say that in the cold war era the security politics of Europe drove the economic relationships. The economic recovery, and then the process of integration, in western Europe was all part of an explicit determination to prevent the West from falling under the influence of Soviet power in the East. Economic relations between eastern and western Europe were entirely driven by the state of the cold war at any one time. The security situation in Europe was the inescapable framework for economic development; both within and between East and West. Between 1945 and 1985 the economic development of Europe simply made no sense if it was not set in its security context.

In the new Europe, however, that relationship seems to have been reversed. The collapse of the Soviet bloc and then the Soviet Union itself owed a great deal to the economic contradictions of their centralised and insensitive economic systems. If the old guard Communist leaderships of Europe felt bewildered at the turn of events after 1988, they could at least have taken comfort in the fact that it was all thoroughly dialectical. Marx would probably have felt he understood it. And now, the security politics of Europe are in a melting pot and being determined, if by anything, then by the ubiquity of economic interdependence which makes the economies of western Europe a political magnet for eastern states. The new states of Europe, and the newly democratic ones, realise that their best

option is to gain entry to this interdependent economic structure
which evolved in one half of Europe during the cold war. The
western states of Europe, on the other hand, realise that their best
option of maintaining peace and political stability throughout
Europe must lie not in offering security guarantees to all and sundry
nor by trying rapidly to extend the Atlantic Alliance to make it into a
type of collective security organisation it has never actually been.
Rather, economic prosperity and the hope of sustained economic
development are regarded as the best recipe for stable governments in
eastern, central and southern Europe, which would then have the
best chances to deal with their ethnic, nationalist, religious and
territorial differences. If ever strategists needed to talk long and hard
with economists and specialists in domestic politics, then it is now.
Good strategists, and for that matter good governments, always did,
of course. But cold war strategy was not a fertile breeding ground for
either.

A second major area in which the student of domestic politics and
of political economy can make important contributions to our understanding of international security in the future arises in the concept of
statehood as an analytical framework. Students of comparative politics have, of late, been considerably less restricted by the concept of
the state as their boundary than was the case in the past. This has not
been universal within comparative politics, but has been led by the
analyses of developments in western European society and also by
the analysis of policy-making in different sectors of modern government. Thanks to its general concentration on western European
politics, the subject has become commendably modern. It has had to
account for government-industry relations when most major
industry is transnational; for macro-economic management when
international arrangements bear critically upon governments' scope
for action over exchange rates, interest rates, or directed subsidies;
for national policy-making when some policy sectors, such as agri-
culture or competition, are controlled from Brussels; and for domestic political trends which in some cases may be critically affected by
what goes on outside the state. The student of comparative politics
has had to grapple with the domestic political impacts of powerful
forces of transnationalism. For comparative politics, the state is not
so obviously the boundary of the relevant 'political community' as it
used to be.

This has an immediate relevance to security politics in Europe in
the ways outlined earlier. Less obviously, however, it should have
relevance to security politics in the world outside the rich members of
the Organisation for Economic Co-operation and Development. To
put it somewhat dramatically, there is a gap in our understanding of
the politics of international security in the South, the Third World or

whatever we choose to call the world of the poor. One of the ironies of the cold war was that its effects seemed to be more persistent in the Third World than they ever were in Europe or in the relations between the United States and the Soviet Union. An East–West dimension – or sometimes a simple anti-Communist dimension – loomed large in many Third World conflicts, allowing policy-makers in the rich world to simplify them sometimes to a reckless degree. Now the cold war is over the poverty of our understanding of conflict in the poor world is painfully clear.

Certainly, the insights of a Martin Wight or a Hedley Bull can give us only a part of the picture. Realists such as these were interested in those patterns of behaviour which could be ascribed to any system of states: that is, to investigate those characteristics that could be regarded as systemic elements in international politics. Their modern examples, not unreasonably, were drawn from the more homogeneous society of states that prevailed in the world during most of the twentieth century about which they were writing. But given that the population of states has expanded both in number and variety since the 1960s, the concept of interstate conflict can tell us only a limited amount about the security problems of some of the most troubled regions of the Third World. The war between Ethiopia and Somalia in the mid-1970s may be explainable in inter-state terms, but that proved to be merely a precursor to a more deeply miserable cycle of conflict, natural disaster and persistent insecurity that has descended on the Horn of Africa region from Sudan to south-east Uganda and northern Kenya. A similar pattern may be discerned in South-East Asia in the years since the Vietnam War. Interstate conflict may have accounted for the tension between China and Vietnam, and that was certainly an element in the international politics of the region, which after the involvement of the United States, suffered the misfortune of becoming the principal arena for the Sino-Soviet dispute. Again, however, competition between states hardly accounts for the extent of present insecurities in Vietnam, Kampuchea, Laos, Burma and even Thailand, rocked as they are by warring guerrilla groups, drug cartels, piracy, refugee movements, and economic deprivation. Something similar could be said about the region that stretches from Central America to the northern section of the Latin American subcontinent. This might be regarded as a region of great international insecurity for rather similar reasons, but international war has been virtually unknown and even the threat of such war has generally been less than credible, notwithstanding tensions over Belize and between El Salvador and Nicaragua.

In all of these regions, the mainsprings of international insecurity are deep and an understanding of those mechanisms that might help to promote security will have to look further than merely interstate

diplomacy or international organisations. The realist model of conflict between states does not do justice to the depth of these security
problems. Neither does the classification of government in an 'underdeveloped' category offered by the comparative politics literature.
This too has done little more than cast Third World politics as
reflections of developed world politics. Clearly, more particular concepts of international security are required when addressing Third
World problems which embody such powerful internal and external,
governmental and non-governmental elements. Such concepts have
somehow to take account of the ways in which external economic
penetration affects political stability: how technology is transferred
from rich to poor countries; how inter-ethnic and economic (or
political) refugee movements affect relations between states; how
non-governmental forces such as multinational companies, not to
mention multinational crime organisations, affect a region; and how
all such forces have an impact on international security. In this
respect the student of politics has something to contribute to a
necessary redefinition of international security. For the future, international security should not be so exclusively regarded as – by
definition – the study of relationships between states. It must, instead, be defined as the study of those forces which affect the
outbreak of violent conflict between any significant groups of people
in the world.

Further, the student of domestic politics – in particular the comparative politics student – can offer the study of international security a better understanding of institutional*ism* in world politics.
International security studies have always been concerned with the
development of institutions such as the United Nations, NATO, the
Warsaw Pact, the Western European Union, the Organisation of
American States, or the Conference on Security and Co-operation in
Europe, as well as the more particular institutions within these
organisations, such as the Independent European Programme Group,
or the Conflict Prevention Centre within the CSCE. The list is long.
But in the confusing world after the cold war the existence of these
security institutions is likely to be less important than the growth of
institutionalised behaviour between states, which is not quite the
same thing. The international institutions which characterised the
cold war era evolved at a glacial pace. In the new world, however,
some institutions have died, others have been created in great haste,
and existing institutions have changed remarkably quickly. Clearly,
the existence of international institutions, as such, will tell us only a
limited amount about the 'architecture of security', or the ways in
which it might serve the security interests of its members, since that
architecture is now being shaped by the behaviour of international
actors who have to face unprecedented circumstances. There is

always a dialectical relationship in the way that institutions shape political behaviour and vice versa. During the cold war the established security institutions formed a well-defined architecture that greatly conditioned the political behaviour of societies and governments throughout the northern hemisphere. Now, however, the balance in the dialectical relationship has shifted a long way and it is the behaviour of powerful states and other economic actors that is determining which institutions will be the most important to the security of the post-cold war world, and how they are likely to relate to each other. The reactions of the major actors to the crises they will face is likely to be highly institutionalised, since they will pursue their objectives through whichever institutions seem likely to yield the best results; but this is probably going to create a somewhat curious form of 'security architecture'. Institutional boundaries will overlap. The competence of different institutions will not be so well understood as it has been, since institutions derive their competence from the commitment their members are prepared to make to them, and institutional evolution will probably continue to be rapid, as more regional and functional organisations proliferate to accommodate the greater diversity posed by newly independent states with diverse social and economic roots.

The study of international security, therefore, needs to understand better the ways in which actors give or withold loyalty to institutions, the ways in which quasi-institutions are formed from recurrent patterns of behaviour, or the ways in which prevailing values can encourage or inhibit institutionalised behaviour. In the most rarified formulation, we might say that the political sociologist and the political behaviouralist should turn the tools of their trade to global society as well as the domestic societies in which most of them specialise. In a more specific formulation we may characterise this point in a number of typical questions for which we must attempt to find acceptable answers. To what extent and in what circumstances, for instance, can international economic institutions supersede a pattern of loyalties based on ethnic or religious groupings in the new states, or newly-democratised states, of Europe? In particular, can the institutions of the European Community, with their links to the other organisations that have promoted peace and prosperity in western Europe, provide a sufficient incentive in east European societies to promote domestic and international behaviour that overrides more obvious ethnic or religious differences? Alternatively, how much of a stake in existing European institutions would eastern European societies require in order to place maintenance of those institutions above more localised security concerns? NATO members have generally perceived themselves to have a very high stake in the Alliance, to which they have subordinated all but the most central of their other security interests. How would such a stake work in the case of eastern European societies? What forms would it take? And how deeply into those societies would an institutional stake have to penetrate in order to have the same social and psychological effect on their views of security as NATO, the EC and the rest have had on ours? Turning away from central and eastern Europe, comparable questions need to be asked of other regions in which 'security architecture' is now an issue. How much does a common Islamic identity weigh against historical state boundaries, or ethnic differences among the societies of Central Asia – the former Asiatic republics of the Soviet Union and some of those in the Middle East – as they attempt to form regional security structures around, say, a 'Caspian Sea Zone'? How much does the Islamic nature of Turkish society and Islamic minorities in southern Europe create an institutional basis for a security structure in southern Europe and the Near East? All such groupings have become a possibility in the post-cold war world, and attempts to bring them to fruition rest on something more complex than a Western realist's view of complementary state interests. To understand it the student of international security needs the help not only of specialists in the domestic politics of those societies, but also of those who understand what makes political institutions work. The fashion for analysing 'international regimes' in the 1970s and 1980s made some inroads into these issues, but hardly sufficient to cope with the plethora of economic and security institutions being touted now, nor the range of relevant international actors who would be involved in them.

It is easier to call for interdisciplinary studies, of course, than to specify how they should work in practice. It is certainly not my contention that the various sub-disciplines of politics – comparative politics, regional studies, political sociology, and so on – are all a single ball of wax that includes international politics. Even if it were true, such an assertion would get us nowhere. But the distinctions that have previously been made between the studies of domestic and international politics, and the use of the state as the boundary which defines both comparative and international politics, are no longer sustainable. Students of these sub-disciplines must be prepared to borrow from each other more than they have in the past. In particular, the student of international security should accept that the subject has been liberated – some would say unleashed – by the end of the cold war which had kept it in blinkers long after the real security agenda in the world had moved on. Studies of both domestic and international politics have to catch up with the fact that the twenty-first century appears to be setting contradictory global trends, where localised sources of political diversity are set against global forces of economic interdependence, and, in some respects, economic integration. Students of both studies will fail to understand what is happening in their chosen world unless they are familiar with what is happening in the other. Perhaps we are back to the situation that applied in academic circles before the First World War, whereby good students of international security – and there were not many – were, *ipso facto*, good students of politics.

The Evolution of the Concept of Security in International Relations

Philip Windsor

I intend to offer a reconsideration of what is meant by security when seen from the standpoint of international relations as a sub-discipline, and indeed of the evolution of what this concept of security has meant.

To begin with, what does one mean by 'evolution' in this context? I would say one can encapsulate it in terms of the relationship between the study of international relations on the one hand and of security on the other, by arguing that a nation's security was once central to the formation of the sub-discipline of international relations, whereas today, it seems to me that the notion of international relations has become central to the definition of security. The study of international relations began as an attempt to think about security, and now in this post-cold war world – where the old structures of the cold war still apply in many respects to the much more chaotic processes by which we still try to define security – some of the central tenets and difficulties of international relations become vital to discussions of future security. So the first part of the analysis must give some consideration at least to the history of international relations.

The Growth of International Relations

International relations is a very peculiar sub-discipline, if, indeed, it can be spoken of as an academic discipline at all. It seems to me that it is in many respects more fruitfully regarded as a cross-roads rather than as an academic discipline – a cross-roads which takes into account various forms of human thought which may range from psychology to law, from anthropology to nuclear strategy, and which at the same time helps us to relate questions arising from those subjects to each other in a way which the traditional demarcation disputes in universities in the past have not enabled us to do. While international relations can equally well draw on the skills and discipline of a physicist and on the reinterpretations and destructuralisations of an anthropologist, nonetheless it does so as a coherent body of thought: in the sense that it addresses the future of humans and their dealings with each other and perhaps even the future of the planet itself. This is not to make it a candidate for some kind of centralised Nobel Prize-winning enterprise which can give answers to highly specific questions and change the future of medicine or something like that – but it is to say that international relations draws together a number of forms and theories of human behaviour which in the past have been studied separately and which now need to be studied in their interactions and their relations with each other.

But it began much more simply. International relations as a sub-discipline of politics was established in the aftermath of the First World War and there is no particular difficulty in understanding why. The First World War destroyed the interrelation of European liberal positivism. The positivists knew what they talked about. Positivists knew what their values were, but they also knew that those values were not related to the facts about which they talked. Positivists knew that the observer stood quite distinct from the observed; the phenomenon which the observer was observing had nothing to do with the person or mind observing it. Positivists knew that there was no distinction between essence and existence. The old kinds of question about what makes a chair a chair were answered by the positivists with retorts like 'Don't be so bloody silly – we all know what a chair is.' The positivists thought they knew the way the universe worked. The positivists also understood that, as we knew more facts, as we understood the world better in its autonomy as a set of phenomena, so actually we became rather nicer people. The argument for this was that with medicine, for example, we could eliminate cholera – in our own time we have eliminated smallpox – with the result that we can conquer the world in which we live. Rationality – with its distinction between fact and value – and the reason of humans in the conduct of their own affairs, became paramount.

The First World War shattered all that. These reasonable, scientific, rational, human beings for whom progress had been a self-evident fact, leading no doubt to value judgement, had been betrayed by events and it became rather important to question why. So the first discussions within a new sub-discipline of politics – the new study of international relations – were in the context of the reactions in many countries, and particularly in the United States, Britain, France and Germany, to the First World War. In other countries, of course, the reaction to that horrific series of events was revolution. But the study of international relations arose in countries where revolution had not occurred, or else had been seen as a legitimate challenge to an existing set of social propositions. International relations, in other words, began as the study of society and of the relations of states in the context of a phenomenon which had been, in a literal sense, incredible. It is significant that in this country, for example, the university chairs of international relations which were established in the aftermath of the First World War were the Montague Burton chairs. Montague Burton was, indeed, a tailor whose name was known on every high street of every major town in the land and hence had sufficient fortune to endow and establish them in the name of his son who had died in the trenches.

The Montague Burton Chairs of International Relations are themselves a kind of memorial to what was both overwhelming in its reality and yet still also conceptually unbelievable. How could we begin to understand the War? In this sense the question of security was, from the beginning, the definitional question that lay at the heart of the study of international relations.

The difficulty, however, was that international relations, both as a sub-discipline and as the conduct of affairs between states, became somewhat problematic within a very few years. The conduct of affairs seemed to suggest that the attempt – much mooted in the League of Nations and proselytised by intellectuals and certain kinds of politician, academics and writers – to wean the world away from the struggle for power between states not only failed but promoted an even greater struggle for power. For those who disarmed, or who were willing to abide by conventions, and those who limited or voluntarily restricted their attempts to impose their will upon others, who did not feel that the act of war could any longer be a legitimate form of conduct of international affairs, simply gave way to those who were prepared to do exactly that.

There is a rather interesting passage in the diary of Count Ciano, Mussolini's Foreign Minister in 1938 at the time of the Munich conference.[1] It was Mussolini who effectively brokered the Munich conference. He thought that Italy would at least get some kudos by sorting out the differences between Germany on the one hand and the major Western powers on the other, dealing with Czechoslovakia in a certain way which pacified the requirements both of immediate international peace and also German territorial and ethnic demands. From Mussolini's point of view, the Munich Conference was very satisfactory. It kept the peace, German demands were met in full – almost – and British and French leaders went away with a settlement. After that conference Ciano recalls in his diary how he strolled along in Munich with Ribbentrop, the German Foreign Minister, and there was Ciano, who was a rather small, dark, pudgy man. Ribbentrop, who was a tall, icy character, walked on, and Ciano trotted after him in the moonlight and said, 'Well, don't you think it's marvellous?'

Ribbentrop stalked on in the darkness, absolutely wracked with fury. Ciano said, 'What's wrong?' and Ribbentrop said, 'We wanted WAR'.

That, unfortunately, is part of the problem. Do the peace-loving attempts to create a system whereby disputes can be resolved – to 'factor war out' of the conduct of international issues – really play into the hands of those who do want war? If one looks at Munich in that respect, it was a temporary defeat for the Third Reich and merely a temporary victory for the ethos behind the study at that time of international relations.

In the period since the Second World War it seems that the sub-discipline which has flourished mightily and has produced many more chairs than those that Montague Burton originally proposed, and a plethora of what is known in the trade as 'the literature', at one stage produced major attempts to change the nature of the discourse. One thinks, for example, of the original Pugwash meetings, meetings at their most respectable between scientists who knew what they were addressing, who worried about the consequences of their own disciplines and who – before Pugwash degenerated into a kind of social science condominium – actually tried to produce an international consensus which moved out from the hard edges of the sciences, particularly that of nuclear physics, to the softer edges of political decision-making. That was part of a process which attempted to internationalise international relations. Equally, other people at this time tried to address the fundamental question of security in terms of articulating stability for the future. But that raised new questions which rapidly destroyed the sub-discipline, or at least its cohesion, and at the same time sharpened the notion of what it is we should try to address.

The only person in those intermediate years after the Second World War who saw the relationship between all these kinds of question, and who moved away from the straightforward power paradigm on the one hand to the rather more complicated questions of what constituted international security on the other – was Raymond Aron.[2] There were no other writers, either in the United States or in Europe, who really tried to encompass these questions.

For the most part the question of security in international relations was really one which broke into several different forms. The first concentrated on the question of 'stability' in the period after the 'avoidance of war' in itself had ceased to seem such a practical and legitimate enterprise. That is to say, that if the avoidance of war had been the primary concern of the period between the two World Wars, and if it had in fact produced, or helped to produce, the catastrophe of the Second World War, then the promotion of war-avoidance had now to take a different form, namely that of imposing stability. And it had to do so through the most horrific and ultimate threat, namely that of nuclear deterrence.

Nuclear deterrence as a manner of imposing stability became a major theme in the study and in the maintenance of international relations both at the conceptual and at the political level. There is an extraordinary symbiosis here between the way that generals argued against politicians in the early years – MacArthur being one notorious example, Curtis E. Le May, perhaps a more fundamental kind of example – and the way academics argued against politicians, saying that we have got to discuss how to avoid a war rather than how to use these weapons. Bernard Brodie was a case in point. Politicians caught in the middle moved increasingly away from the idea that wars can be won towards the idea that stability could be imposed.

So in one sense the paradigm of conduct in the real world of international politics and the study of that conduct, and then the furtherance of the sub-discipline of international relations, all became increasingly involved with the question of 'What constitutes stability?' Stability, it was naturally assumed, constitutes 'security', and security was therefore equated with the 'permanently operating factors', to coin a phrase of that era, which defined the way that nuclear deterrence worked.

Now did it? Was that so? There are so many questions wherein we might engage in an almost medieval disputation about this. Can we expect nuclear deterrence to work as a fixed paradigm for the future? Such questions have technical components where they relate to probability theory. Could we really tie ourselves to a definite form of probabilism for an unknown time with an unknown number of factors? Was, in other words, the study of international relations getting stuck in a form of security which tied itself to an increasingly uncertain system called nuclear deterrence? And if this was unacceptable, were there other ways of going about the business of security? The late 1950s witnessed a kind of bifurcation developing between the 'stability equals security equals nuclear deterrence' proponents on the one hand, and the 'we'd better change the human race' proponents on the other, who were dedicated to the re-education of human political behaviour.

My own interpretation would be that it is extremely difficult to tie either of these approaches successfully to the question of what constitutes security. Security cannot be defined as a straightforward calculation of military risks. It cannot be defined in terms of the durability of a stable nuclear deterrent system. It cannot be defined in terms of technological innovation which more or less produces a more or less stable arms race, which more or less 'factors out' the alternative risks of one side to the arms control calculations of the other.

Arms control, for example, is sometimes regarded as a form of stabilised deterrence, as a way of saying, 'Well, within our different modes we are both trying to approach the same goal even though we face different problems'. But arms control might also be a way of stimulating arms races, of introducing certain difficulties in political discourse, of making it *more* difficult to define security rather than less. Take, for instance, the question of arms control verification. We would all presumably agree that verification is a necessary part of the arms control process both for the purpose of arriving at limitation and also simply to ensure that nobody is cheating. But there is a paradox inherent in verification. If one asks why we have to verify in the first place; the answer would presumably be, 'Because at least at the beginning of the process of arms control, of limitation and even perhaps reduction, we don't actually trust each other. We want to check'. So verification is, in the first instance, a mutual acceptance of common distrust. One might very well say that, in that case, mutual acceptance of common distrust, resolved through the process of verification, is not a bad idea. It solves many problems and helps to get us a bit further down the road to peace. But then there are the technicalities. What do we verify? What are we looking at? What do we need to see before we know whether a system is actually being reduced or immolated? We would like to check whether such-and-such a cruise missile or such-and-such a submarine is carrying a nuclear or a conventional warhead. We need to know what a particular weapon system looks like, how heavy it is going to be, what the total load is, how the gyros work, how one puts in the cassettes, the radar maps, and so on. This is called, in the terms of the trade, 'intrusive verification' and the more you want to verify the more the other party has to trust you. In other words, 'The more I distrust you, the more you have to trust me. Because I distrust you I want all your secrets. The only way you can give me all your secrets is by trusting me to deal with them responsibly, seriously and decently'. So intrusive verification, in fact, maximises distrust and yet demands maximisation of trust on the other hand.

How then are we to deal with these problems? The answer is that we cannot deal with them through an arms control process alone. There has to be a basis of political confidence or political exchange. Arms control only 'works' when the political circumstances between the parties to an agreement are favourable. This means the end to the military autonomy: to the purely strategic definition of security. It means that we can no longer define security except in terms of the wider concerns of international relations, and that those wider concerns cannot be confined only to the areas of political decision-making or political control. This means that in turn – and this is where the question of security in international relations becomes extremely difficult – we have to ask whether we are simply talking about security between states, or rather security in the context of all those other difficult questions raised by the concepts of 'world society', 'community', individuals at various levels of society, 'common concerns', and so on.

The argument here, in other words, is that the evolution of the question of security in terms of the sub-discipline of international relations, having been defined primarily in military and strategic terms because of the reaction to the First World War, having gone through a rather terrible period of evolution in attempts to get away from it between the two World Wars, and having then gone through a redefinition in military-strategic terms in the nuclear politics of the cold war, the definition of security has now found itself ineluctably pushed to the point where the very conditions of security have to be further defined by our relations on a global scale.

The elegant simplicity of the vanished cold war one might come to regret. It might have been true to say that for a certain historical period the world was somewhat calmer – and perhaps a little less subject to the whims of well-armed psychopaths than it is now. One could also construct a strong historical argument, for example, that Saddam Hussein who so troubled the world of the 1990s, was very much a product of the exporting of cold war tension to other regions and societies. Nevertheless, whether one regrets the passing of cold war elegances or whether one regards the contemporary world as partly a product of them, it remains the case that for the rest of the 1990s neither strategic studies, nor peace studies, nor studies of human society, or whatever, have given us much of a working definition of security, or offered an approach to security in terms of the new political relations which are emerging in the world.

Criteria for a New Definition of Security

We therefore have to reconsider what we mean by security in the contemporary study of international relations. We might begin by stepping back to ask 'whose security?' Is it the security of states that we are concerned with? If so, we still have to question the purpose of states. Are states a repository of values in which, in 1990 for example, the values of the state of Iraq went to war with the values of the state of Kuwait, and, in 1991, of the Republic of the United States of America? Are we, on the other hand, talking about states as some kind of undetermined actor in which values become anonymous? One of the conclusions we might draw from the 1990-91 Gulf War is that it is impossible to regard states at war as morally neutral and yet equally impossible to regard states as moral actors. The state system, therefore, comes into question when we are talking about a greater international agreement on security. And yet the study of international relations, despite attempts to suggest an alternative, has until now been focused on the state, and it could not be otherwise. It is extraordinary when one considers the activities of multinational companies, various international movements, the Catholic Church, terrorist groups, and so on, just how powerful the state remains. It is extraordinary that the tin pot dictator of a Mickey Mouse state, such as Colonel Gaddafi, can nationalise, for example, Occidental Petroleum. The United States is not prepared, as a state, to go to war to defend Occidental Petroleum and all the other companies operating in Libya. But the situation would be different if it were. The state, in other words, is extremely instrumental, if not powerful, in defining how the international system shall work at any given moment. If states choose to fight, there will be international conflict; if not, then a form of international peace will prevail, whatever the inner conflicts within the global system.

But how do we deal with the state? There is a problem. For the state is, in a sense, stuck in a position which Hegel suggested a long time ago. Now Hegel, of course, was in many ways a champion of the state. Hegel regarded it as a vehicle for the world spirit. But Hegel's admiration of the state contradicts what I think is the central thrust of his own argument in what I regard as his masterpiece, '*The Phenomenology of the Spirit*'.[3] He suggests a parable involving two conflicting characters, the future master and the future slave. At the moment when they come into conflict they are only contingent beings and they engage in a fight that could be to the death. They have a choice to make: namely, that given that they are contingent, and that the survival of their minds and their wills depends on the survival of their bodies, they must decide whether the body is to be preserved so they can go on thinking, or whether the mind will refuse to sacrifice its liberty, its will, its decision, even at the risk of death. The Hegelian dilemma has been well-encapsulated in a much more modern catchphrase which was prevalent in the 1950s and 1960s, namely the discussion as to which was preferable: 'better Red than dead', or else 'better dead than Red'.

In Hegel's view the person who transcends the contingent, the one who says, 'I would rather die than sacrifice the independence of my mind', and who is therefore prepared to die, will triumph over the one who is prepared to sacrifice independence of mind in order to preserve the existence of the organism. So the latter, the one who is more likely to surrender, becomes the slave, and the former, who is prepared to die rather than risk the independence of mind, becomes the master. But where Hegel is so brilliant is where he then suggests that now the master is historically stuck. The master cannot progress any further, because from now on the master's mastery is based on the acquiescence of the slave, and if the slave decides one day 'I am not going to obey you. Kill me if you like', or more likely if the slave's grandchildren so decide, then that is the end of the master's power. Power, in Hegel's terms, is something not that one has but rather that other people give one, and the minute they decide not to, the game is over. The Shah of Iran discovered that.

Equally, Hegel argues, the master has an alternative approach, which is not to try to coerce the slave through fear but instead to ask for the slave's co-operation. This is what Hegel calls 'desiring the other's desire'. But, of course, if you desire the other's desire, you are no longer master. So in either case the master is historically finished. The future is in the hands of the slave. Now it seems to me – this is why I think it contradicts Hegel's view of the state – that the state is precisely stuck in the position of the master. If it tries to coerce with raw power it ultimately fails. The United States has found this to be the case in the present era and in a previous era many an imperialist country could attest to the same thing.

One cannot coerce the co-operation of others; it depends on their own interpretation of their situation. Equally, of course, since the state system is built on some definition of power, once the state 'desires the other's desire' we are beginning to talk about the deconstruction of the state system. In this peculiar historical transition – the post-cold war world – it seems that we are living through a period in which the deconstruction of state power is in many ways going ahead very rapidly. Yet we have still not arrived at a point where we can say with any confidence that there is agreement in the world in social, humanitarian, global terms, on the fundamental purposes of international co-operation, or the rationale of international security. Yet such questions are exactly the central concerns of the sub-discipline of international relations.

World politics is not, however, in a good position to develop new criteria for the understanding of such questions in the present era. The security relationship, for example, between the North/South axis and the East/West axis raises questions which the study of international relations has handled badly indeed. The Brandt Report – in the good old days – argued quite strongly that, in fact, unless we redressed the questions of justice and order in North/South relations we were going to have tremendous East/West conflict. This argument was a massive *non sequitur*. If the Third World disappeared tomorrow, I doubt that many people in the West or the East would notice it. Indeed, two of the co-authors of the Brandt Report subsequently agreed with me that there was 'no relationship whatsoever' between North/South and East/West security. 'But', they said in a private conversation, 'we thought we'd better put it in because we didn't believe that the audience in the West would accept the moral criteria, so we tried to make them practical'.

What, therefore, do we mean by 'security'? What do we mean by the relationship between the internal security of certain societies and the external security of their neighbours, their ex-opponents, or their current protagonists or fellow protagonists in the system? This has come up very clearly in the crisis occasioned by the collapse of the Soviet Union, and the implications of its collapse for the rest of us. It was a fact that the criteria of internal security in the Soviet Union was being sacrificed to the criteria of *perestroika* and reform.

If security values are sacrificed to *perestroika* the effect could be disastrous. So the old criteria, by which we judged the presence and degree of security in the system, have gone. We are, in fact, not only in a period of extraordinarily complicated political transition but also in a period of highly conflicting intellectual criteria. The study of the conflicts of those criteria might be one of the ways in which we have to re-approach both the definition of international relations and the definition of security.

In this context it is highly appropriate that we remember the work of the late John Vincent, because that was an extended argument, as I see it, for the ability to apply the study of reason to the study of human values, and to engage in the study of international relations as a whole on a more global scale than that which had been undertaken hitherto. In that sense it would seem to me that, drawing inspiration from him, our fundamental concern should now be to engage in a dialogue of values and possibly in a genuine dialogue between cultures over the meaning of security for our future.

NOTE

This lecture was originally to be given by Professor John Vincent of the Department of International Relations, London School of Economics. His sudden death was a great loss to the academic profession, and in particular to international politics in Britain. Philip Windsor agreed to give a lecture in his place. He dedicates the lecture to the memory of John Vincent, in the knowledge that the approach he adopts here was close to the heart of his colleague and friend.

Economics and Security:
The Disciplines and the Reality

Ron Smith

At conferences on military matters, I have noticed two phenomena. The first is the number of times that the importance of economics to security is emphasised. I want to examine some of those cases where economics is important to security and to look at the way that they interact. There are a lot of examples. At the systemic level there is the contribution of military spending to the rise and fall of great powers; at the international level there is the extent to which economics should be used to meet security objectives and vice versa; at the domestic level there is the emphasis that should be given to military and industrial factors in the maintenance of a national defence industrial base. These sorts of issue are the reality of my title.

But at these conferences I notice a second phenomenon. Having emphasised the importance of economic questions, the speakers make a dash for the doors as soon as economists try to answer them. Nothing clears a security conference hall faster than a group of economists getting down to discussing the relative price effect and the like. I often feel that we are like the computer in *The Hitchiker's Guide to the Galaxy*. It was constructed to answer the question of 'life, the universe and everything'. It came out with the answer, which as you probably know, is 42. The audience found the answer somewhat unsatisfactory, not quite what they had been expecting, not sure how it answered the question they posed. I think that many in the security community have that sort of response to the answers economists give: What is this to do with security? That is the problem of the disciplines of my title.

I want to use an example from my own teaching to make a general point about the interaction of economics and security studies. There is a fairly arcane and technical piece of statistics that is very important in economics: it is the theory of censored and truncated probability distributions. To soften my students up for the algebra, I tell them where the theory came from. It was developed by Abraham Wald, who, during the Second World War, was given the job of advising the American military on where the armour should be put on bombers. Weight considerations meant that only a limited amount could be used, to protect the critical parts, and there was considerable dispute among the engineers about which parts of the aircraft were critical. Many would regard it as a matter of common sense what the critical parts were. He did not treat it so, but as a matter for systematic analysis.

First he assembled all the data on the bullet holes in returning aircraft. These, of course, were the wrong data. What he needed was the data on the bullet holes in aircraft that did not return. So he invented a whole new branch of statistics, developing a model (by model I mean a set of equations) for the distribution of bullets over all aircraft, returning and non-returning. This provided the basis for a set of procedures for using the data you do observe to make inferences about what are not observed, because the data are censored or truncated for some specified reason. Wald was a statistician rather than an economist, but the process is similar to the one we use. Collect the data you can, construct a formal model which explains what you know and use that as a basis for inference and policy judgements about what you do not know. As a result of the importance that they attach to the model as providing a formal framework, economists tend to reverse the engineers' dictum that 'that's all very well in theory but does it work in practice?' We are more likely to say, 'that's all very well in practice, but does it work in theory?' This is because, unless we have a good model – a theory that explains what happens, we will not know what are the possible outcomes of a given policy, and we will not know how to choose between contending policies. However, the computerised analysis of data and the mathematical framework, which are central to this process, are also obstacles to communication.

As evidence of what people say at conferences about the importance of economics, I shall quote a summary of a conference reviewing international security studies, given by Joseph S. Nye and Sean M. Lynn-Jones.[1] They say, 'The division between the fields of international political economy and international security is one of the most serious problems within the discipline of political science . . . As a result economic dimensions of security have received short shrift.' This extract is interesting because it has a subtext, which embodies academic border disputes that rival the Schleswig-Holstein question.

First, they do not regard international security studies as a discipline, rather it is a problem area, a field within the discipline of political science. I understand international security to be the study of the use, threat and control of force in the relations between states: the interaction of military capability and international relations. I am using a narrow definition of security, and it seems to me that there are enough well-established analytical techniques in this area, some of them provided by economists like Schelling, that it is sensible to call it a discipline, but I do not insist on this.

Secondly, they emphasise the division between two fields within political science: international political economy and international security; not the relation with a quite different discipline, economics. The growth of the field of international political economy within political science raises some interesting questions. Susan Stange puts this clearly in the introduction to the edited collection *Paths to International Political Economy*, which has contributions from a range of disciplines.[2] She emphasises how open a field international political economy is; academics from any discipline may contribute, except economists. Economists cannot contribute, she says, because of their rigidity and unwillingness to answer questions in any but their own terms. I think that there is great truth in this criticism, but it arises largely because the questions international political economy wants to answer are political questions. They are about international economic issues certainly; but they are not the economic questions about the international economic issues that economists want to answer. There are some economists who are good at handling the political aspects, but not many, and they are mainly in the United States rather than in Britain. Efficient division of labour would suggest that the political analysis should be left to international relations and political science specialists.

The third aspect of the quotation from Nye and Lynn-Jones is their concern with the economic dimensions of security. It has been recently fashionable to emphasise the wider dimensions of security: environmental security, economic security, social security even. I am rather sceptical about these wider dimensions, not because I think that the substantive issues such as the greenhouse effect, the debt crisis, or child benefit are unimportant, far from it; they are crucial, but they are not about 'security' as security specialists understand it. I cannot see the comparative advantage that someone with the disciplinary skills appropriate for the analysis of arms control talks, the START Treaty or nuclear warhead design and 'power projection' brings to these issues. In fact, I can see ways in which the transfer of security preconceptions would be counterproductive. While it would be cynical and overly materialist to say that the sudden concern with the wider dimensions of security was a response by people who thought that the end of a cold war had put them out of a job, economists do not mind being thought cynical and overly materialist.

In passing, I do not intend to discuss 'economic security', because I have no idea what the term means in this context. What I would call economic security, the standard deviation of the present discounted value of the random variable future utility, is not the sort of thing that the 'wider dimensions' community had in mind; and were I to start talking standard deviations of present values, then I would certainly clear the hall. So I am interested in economics and in military security and how they interact. These questions are very complicated. We simplify them by using disciplined structures of analysis to provide windows on reality, limited and partial views. So I am interested in demonstrating how that interaction is viewed through the economist's window on the world.

Economics is usually defined as something like 'the study of the allocation of scarce resources between competing ends,' or of the process of production, distribution and exchange. I became interested in defence and have been kept interested in defence primarily by the fact that there is a lot of money involved. One of the difficulties in communicating with people is that the sums of money involved are so large that you quite quickly lose track of the odd billion here and there. For the cost of *Trident* you could have bought one and a half Channel tunnels, had you also wanted half a Channel tunnel. What distinguishes economists, however, beyond their fixation on money, is the way they approach the questions. Economists like formal systems and a chain of deductive reasoning; they like to structure the problem consistently within an explicit accounting and measurement system; to get well-defined questions which they can answer with their well-developed technical tools. Our inclination is to count, model and optimise, to operationalise the question. These are useful skills; the Centre for Defence Studies, for example, got a lot of publicity for the numbers its economist produced on the cost of the Gulf War. But it does produce a prejudice towards things that can be quantified, an inclination to over-simplify in order to produce a mathematically-tractable model, and a tendency to impute rationality where it is inappropriate. Many of my friends think that imputing rationality to anything connected with the military is completely inappropriate, but I disagree and continue to use optimising models. The nicest – that is, the most precise, if not the most pleasant – critique of the mistakes that an economic perspective can induce is by Edward Luttwak in his call for more 'waste, fraud and mismanagement' in the Pentagon.[3] Compared with the Pentagon, the Ministry of Defence in Britain has largely managed to exclude economists; but the general issue of the materialist bias that Luttwak identifies is as important here.

Bearing our biases in mind, I want to look at some of the ways that the national economy will influence British security in the 1990s. Sam Goldwyn said never make prophecies, particularly about the future, and forecasting, as defence analysts know, is a fool's game.

To operationalise security we have to start with the threat, the enemy. Over some years of watching the Ministry of Defence, I have noticed that they respond to three serious enemies; these are the enemies who shape security decisions. These do not include anyone we actually go to war with, such as the Irish, the Iraqis and the Argentinians; and in this list of enemies, the Soviets ranked a clear third. There is no doubt who enemy number one is, the opponent whom the Ministry really puts its effort into fighting: it is the Treasury. This battle with the Treasury is the first way that the economy will shape security in the 1990s: the dialectical interaction between the state of the economy and military spending, mediated through the public expenditure battles between the Ministry and the Treasury.

For the last four decades the imbalances between policy, programme and budget have provided the dynamic that has shaped British security policy, and I see no reason why that tension should stop. This is an area that has been extensively analysed, and I do not want to repeat the obvious. However, when I boot up my computer and start projecting military spending for the late 1990s, using equations that have worked out in the past, the numbers that come out are substantially lower in real terms than at present, and constitute around 2.5 per cent of GDP. This continues the recent trend. The share of GDP devoted to defence has dropped from 5.3 per cent in 1938–84 to about 3.8 per cent in 1989–90, the lowest since the 1930s, and the trend is likely to continue. Whatever happens in the 1990s the dissolution of the Soviet Union and the Warsaw Pact and the unification of Germany have reduced the threat on the central front. The Ministry's 'Options for Change' process did not resolve the tensions, and more hard choices seem likely. Nor do I think that the Gulf War has fundamentally changed the judgement as to 'How much is enough?' though it may cause us to downgrade our estimate of the threat posed by former Soviet weapons and the quantitative superiority they fomerly enjoyed. The problems within the defence programme are well known: the overheads needed to maintain small forces are very high; the cuts may push forces below threshold levels of viability; the cost of weapons grows much faster than inflation; and the characteristics for a less well-defined security environment, such as mobility and flexibility, are inordinately expensive. There were substantial efficiency gains in the defence budget in the late 1980s, but the potential national improvements are largely exhausted; further gains require international actions. These are all well-worn paths.

Whereas my first economic influence on security policy – the interaction of Britain's poor economic performance with the rising costs of commitments – was parochial, the second – economic integration – is global. The dominant force of the period since the

Second World War, has been increased economic integration characterised by falling costs of transport and communication; the rapid
growth of trade and a new international division of labour; the
spread of multinational companies which integrate production at a
regional and global level; the opening of financial markets so that
vast amounts of money flow from country to country simply on
rumour. The Single European Market will reinforce these well-
established trends within Europe. Whether you call it interdependence, internationalisation of capital, or globalisation of the economy, economic integration is a major force shaping culture, politics
and security. The political implications, particularly the loss of
autonomy by national governments, are obvious, but defence
remained remarkably immune to the pressures of internationalism
for a long time. I think defence will be influenced in these developments much more in the 1990s, partly because of the internationalisation of the industry that supplies them, partly because economic
integration is driving political integration, where European interests
are supplanting national interests, and partly because no European
country will be able to afford viable force structures without multilateral integration.

Unlike other industries, where the dominant structure was one of
competing multinationals, the arms industry was characterised by
protected national monopolies locked in symbiotic relations with
their host governments. That pattern is changing. From the mid-
1980s, the falling defence budgets, the 30 to 40 per cent excess of
capacity in the industry, the diseconomies of very short national
production runs, and the inefficiencies associated with politically
motivated, bureaucratically organised collaborative projects,
together produced sufficient tension to shift the equilibrium. The
wave of company mergers, acquisitions and divestments was driven
by factors clearly apparent before the end of the cold war. The
ending of the cold war has still to be fully factored into the arms
business's industrial decisions. The recent shifts in industry structure
may prefigure a more normal market of a few big internationally-
integrated, multinational producers, or else a widescale exit which
will leave Europe with no international competitors, just a few,
heavily-subsidised, inefficient, national producers. A major obstacle
to restructuring is the concern with maintaining an illusory facade of
national self-sufficiency. We may continue to call a weapon British or
American, but whatever the flag, the bits inside it are likely to have
come from all over the world.

Because economic processes operate at supranational levels, they
need to be regulated at supranational levels. Capital adequacy ratios
for banks have to be agreed internationally and competition policy
has to operate at, as a minimum, a European level. As a result,

national interests and sovereignty become less well-defined. Britain has major economic interests in common with Europe and can only advance them in conjunction with Europe. Even where the interests do not exactly coincide, as in agricultural policy, it is still better for our interests to negotiate in the General Agreement on Tariffs and Trade as part of the European Community, maintaining a unified alliance against the USA, than to go it alone.

A driving force in integration is that economies of scale require large enterprises. It is surprising that in the area where such economies are most marked, the military, there has been the most resistance to the formation of large enterprises. Despite Voltaire's inside information that God was on the side of the big battalions, Europe has insisted on maintaining lots of little battalions, justifying their effectiveness by special bilateral relationships with the USA. The imbalance between our economic alliances and military alliances is very striking.

But this brings us back to the serious enemies of the Ministry of Defence. Number three was the Soviets, Number one was the Treasury, Number two is undoubtedly the French. Lord Raglan was not the last British general to think of our allies the French being the enemy rather than the Russians. But European defence co-operation must rest on the resolution of Anglo-French differences; not, however, on a bilateral basis but on the construction of multilateral forces. Bilateral deals, as with a new stand-off missile, are peripheral to the building of European forces. To say that such co-operation must rest on Anglo-French agreement is too strong; there are alternative routes and monetary co-operation provides a model. The British and the French were never able to resolve their differences over monetary co-operation. But both eventually, and very reluctantly in the case of Britain, had to accept the alternative, which was German, or rather *Bundesbank* hegemony over their monetary policies. The French and the smaller countries see that in many respects a European central bank and a European currency give them more autonomy than the present system, where they have to follow Germany. Britain is slowly following this line of thought. While the *Bundeswehr* is the biggest army in Europe, as yet it does not have the authority of the *Bundesbank*, but it may come, and the Germans could inherit the American roles in the NATO Integrated Military Command.

This is silly speculation, prophecies of the sort that Sam Goldwyn warned against. But to an economist, it is a very natural sort of speculation. Economic structures are much more flexible, they change steadily, there is a moving equilibrium, so to extrapolate trends and relationships is a natural way to work. Political structures are much more rigid, the strains get too much, they crack and the system moves to a completely different equilibrium. It is the common, unquestioned beliefs, the things that are taken for granted, which keep an equilibrium stable. There are given political truths, such as that French troops cannot serve under foreign officers, which provide the parameters of discourse.

But as we have seen, those truths are transitory, and when the political equilibrium moves, it moves quickly, making it difficult to predict. Two years ago, any prophecies which correctly predicted the political turn of events after 1989 would have appeared as simply preposterous. But the economic forces behind those changes were a standard topic of discussion: the damage the Soviet military burden was doing to its economy; the inefficiency of the planning system; the dangers of arms exports, high military burdens and the inequitable distribution of income in the Middle East. But drawing political implications is difficult, and as a result there are sensible bounds on speculation in normal political discourse which there are not in economic discourse. Thus I find it slightly disconcerting going from a security conference, where the trivia of sovereignty are given great weight ('Britain will not be a nation without a tank industry') to economic conferences, where enemy number one, the Treasury, is seriously talking to enemy number two, the French, about abolishing the most fundamental symbol of national sovereignty, the national currency. And economists are busily calculating the costs and benefits of the change.

The final economic process I want to outline is income inequality. Europe is rich and is surrounded by poor countries, from eastern Europe to the Maghreb. There are obvious tensions produced by this inequality – political instability, migration pressures, disputes over resources such as water – and these tensions will exacerbate nationalist, ideological and religious divisions. It is difficult to build political success on economic failure, and there is a real danger that Europe's borders will remain scattered with economic failures. Primarily this is an economic problem, to be dealt with by economic policies, but political and military responses may be needed.

Thus I think that economic performance, integration and inequality will shape security concerns in the 1990s, and I think that economists have something to offer in analysing them. But let us not forget that economists tend to see these problems differently from the security community. So before you flee the conference hall next time, remember that the economist is looking at the world through spectacles of equations and formal models, and sees a world where the balance of power is quite different. Whom the military regard as strong, the USA and Russia, we see as basket cases; and whom the military regard as weak, Germany and Japan, we see as the dominant powers. Where students of international security see international institutions as peripheral to national interests, economists see such institutions, particularly multinational companies and financial markets, and even the European Community, as having removed a large part of national autonomy. Thus it is no wonder that our answers sound like '42'.

War and the Nation-State: Retrospect and Prospect

Christopher Dandeker

This title has been chosen for two reasons: first, although there is a fairly well established field of research in the sociology of the military or armed forces and society, this has developed very much away from the mainstream of thinking and research. Modern sociology has tended to steer clear of the institutional problems of war and military power; yet it is plain that in order to understand the nature and prospects of nation-states – the building blocks of the modern world and key problems of sociology – war and military power must be central themes in that investigation.

In my own work in social theory and the sociology of armed forces, I have tried to place war and military power more centre-stage on the contemporary sociological agenda, as have a number of other sociologists. In the United Kingdom, two in particular come to mind: Michael Mann and Anthony Giddens.[1] This has involved reasserting (although not uncritically) the claims of what I have called neo-Machiavellian social theory (what others have called conservative or neo-realist), against the predominant paradigms of Marxism and the liberal theory of industrial society as found in the works of Comte, Durkheim, and Spencer. Sociologists, in other words, have paid insufficient attention to war and military power, even though this theme is a crucial part of the answer to key problems of their discipline: the nature of and the prospects for the modern nation-state.

My second reason is to deal with the claim that the first reason no longer really applies: the mini-renaissance of the sociology of war and military power in the late 1980s is now outdated. That is to say, war and military power focused on the modern nation-state are of declining relevance in the increasingly globalised, interdependent planet which we inhabit. With the death of Communism and the emergent hegemony of the values of market capitalism and liberal democracy it has been argued by Fukuyama that we are witnessing perhaps 'the end of history' or the extension of what Charles Moskos has called a 'warless society'[2]. Neither of these authors has suggested that we should expect the growth of a warless planet. Rather, war and military power will have relevance more for the relations between the developed capitalist world and the underdeveloped nations than for relations amongst the developed powers themselves; and, moreover, the community of the latter is likely to grow and take in more of the planet as we head into the twenty-first century. Thus in the relations between developed and developing nations, with the death of Communism it can be argued that the prospects for the spread of liberal capitalism look brighter. The use of force against regional dictators who stand in the way of the triumph of liberal values will continue to be necessary, but this can take place under the aegis of an international community no longer riven by the bipolar superpower conflict, and indeed guaranteed militarily if not economically by the only superpower, the USA. The developed powers themselves have now and will have even less reason in the future to resort to military means to resolve disputes with those who are economically and politically rather like themselves. Winners and losers there will continue to be but these will be selected by 'soft' social and economic power mechanisms not 'hard' military ones, and their interrelations will increasingly be constrained and mediated by supranational organisations. The 200-year-old reign of the sovereign nation-state is drawing to a close. With some qualification then, the claims of liberal social theory in the nineteenth century were right: they were just stated a little prematurely.

Modernity: a world of Nation-States

When one surveys the modern era from a sociological point of view, four 'clusters of modernity' may be identified. In brief they are:

1. The establishment of a durable state administration based on a centralised control of the means of violence and a dramatic expansion in the destructive capacities of military power.
2. Goods and services are produced and distributed in an economic system centred on the large-scale business enterprise. In capitalism, now more hegemonic than ever before, the operations of the enterprise are mediated by the disciplines of the market place.
3. Co-ordination of the division of labour in the economic and other spheres of society is facilitated by the use of rational technologies. Industrial technologies based on mechanical and electromechanical processes are increasingly being supplanted by post-industrial or electronic processes and are centred more and more on information rather than on hard goods.

4. In the co-ordination of the formal organisations of modern societies, and especially of those which are crucial for the reproduction of power – the state and business enterprise-rational bureaucracy is the key administrative instrument.

Now it is through the conjoining of these institutional clusters that modern 'societies' have emerged: that is to say, as Anthony Giddens has suggested, societies are actually products of modernity. If by 'society' we mean a clearly demarcated and internally well-articulated social entity, it is only relatively recently that large human populations have lived under such arrangements and these have been the achievements of modern nation-states. From a political point of view, the modern world comprises a network of competing nation-states and collectivities aspiring to that status.[3]

Modern nation-states have well-developed bureaucratic systems for the internal policing of their populations as well as for the management of their external relations. Their systems of rule are legitimated in terms of the politics of citizenship and the bonds of national solidarity, although, of course, many nation-states are multi-ethnic or multi-national units.

As Bendix has argued, 'the central fact of modern nation building is the orderly exercise of a nation-wide public authority'.[4] Four key aspects of this political transformation may be noted here: first, the concentration of political authority; secondly, the extension of citizenship rights – civil, political and social; thirdly, the administrative instruments of power of the modern state become the property of the public rather than being privately owned by the monarch. The impersonal public authority of the state entails an institutional separation between state and society. The administrative functions of government become 'removed from the political struggle in the sense that they cannot be appropriated on a hereditary basis by privileged estates and on that basis parcelled out among competing jurisdictions'.[5] And finally, the fourth dimension of the modern nation-state concerns its surveillance capacities: rational bureaucracy is the means of penetrating society in order to gather resources and supervise the population. While the modern state is separated from society in respect of the emergence of a public power from pre-existing patrimonial regimes, from an administrative or surveillance point of view, pre-modern states and their rulers were far more separated from their societies than are their modern counterparts. The former could not subject their populations to the fine mesh of bureaucratic surveillance evident in modern states. One of the major, albeit relative, contrasts between pre-modern and modern states is that in the latter there is an emergent division between external and internal relations together with a corresponding specialisation of bureaucratised military power on the one hand and police surveillance on the other. The corollary of a predominantly externally-facing military organisation is a pacified domestic population. In the domestic sphere, the population does not, as a matter of routine, provide sources of collective armed opposition to the central authorities. On this basis of internal pacification, and bureaucratised military power, modern states can behave like actors in the network of international relations, which is itself a distinct feature of modernity.

War, Military Power and the Emergence of Modern Nation-States

Although war and military power have been crucial influences in the development of modern societies as nation-states, they have not been given the attention they deserve in the discipline of sociology. Why? This is because the two pre-eminent traditions of social theory are characterised by reductionist accounts of war and military power. Proponents both of the liberal theory of industrial society and of Marxism argue that war and the importance of military power will decline with the maturation of modern societies. For the former, the development of the division of labour in and between societies will ensure that peaceful activities of production and exchange will supplant warfare. The networks of global interdependence established by market exchange provide conditions under which a peaceful concert of nation-states can thrive. War will no longer be required because the global market provides a means of removing the main cause of war – scarcity of economic resources. Aggressive nationalism will wane with the rise of a united humanity and the triumph of reason over tradition and emotion. So argued Comte, Durkheim, Spencer, Cobden and Bright. In contrast, Marxist social theory regards war and military power as aspects of the political struggle in class societies. Far from being a constitutive feature of a world of competing states, war is contingent upon the existence of class divisions. Socialising the means of production and thus abolishing class divisions, preferably on a world scale, would remove the socio-economic basis of war between societies and military organisation within societies, prefacing the establishment of a peaceful confederation of nation-states. Thus this view constitutes a mirror image of the liberal vision to be found in the theory of industrial society: for the Marxist, the capitalist market is the root of war, while for the Liberal, so long as it is conjoined with the politics of liberal democracy, it is the basis of peace.[6]

In contrast with these two traditions, the Machiavellian strand of social theory as found in the writings of Gumplowicz, Weber, Hintze and Elias (all heavily influenced by the geopolitical wranglings of central and eastern Europe in the late nineteenth and the early twentieth century) focused on the importance of the state as a warlike entity and were reluctant to view human conflicts as being rooted in economic scarcity. Rather, they regarded human conflicts as part of the human condition, because of instinctive aggression and territorial imperatives, or competing absolute values, and thus as resistant to any corrosive effects of modernity. War and military power, it has to be admitted, are thus here to stay! The argument is not that this third strand of social theory should be accepted uncritically, but rather it suggests that the wisest course would be to synthesise the insights of each of these intellectual traditions. The importance of this Machiavellian tradition is that it sensitises us to the impact of war and military power on the development of modern societies as nation-states. This point may be illustrated as follows:

First, warfare played a central part in the genesis of the infrastructure of the early modern European state as a territorially-bounded agency, both separate from society and equipped with bureaucratic means for supervising its own population. The dominant concern of the early modern state and its principal item of expenditure related to the mobilisation of resources in the pursuit of power, chiefly by means of war with other emerging states. In Europe the foundations of the modern state were forged in wars which stemmed from a peculiarly intense level of rivalries amongst the component parts of a pluralistic geopolitical and cultural system.

Secondly, as war was a major and persistent feature of the early modern and the modern state, military organisations were normally at the leading edge of bureaucratic development: the development of professional officer corps, military discipline, divisional forms of control – all later found their echo in the business world, thus revealing the error in those arguments – Marxist and otherwise – which stress the primacy of capitalism in generating these administrative developments so distinctive of the modern world.

Thirdly, war not only led to the development of bureaucratised military organisations but also to an extension of the state's supervisory activities over society for military objectives. There were two broad phases in this development: to begin with, the formation of professional military organisations; then the mobilisation of national citizenries into large, bureaucratic, mass military organisations as a result of the industrial and the democratic revolutions. This was a fairly drawn-out and uneven process stretching from the end of the eighteenth century through to the two World Wars of the twentieth century. National citizenries were mobilised by states in a variety of relatively civilianised liberal or militarised autocratic systems, ranging from the United States to Germany, Japan and Russia. This wave even engulfed societies like Britain in 1916, and then during and after the Second World War. The pressures of war and the political desire for military effectiveness certainly stimulated many societies to modernise their social structures in relation to industrial development and the extension of citizenship on liberal or authoritarian lines. Without a mass armed force owing allegiance to the democratised nation-state many societies were doomed to second-class status, or worse. Such calculations played a crucial part in the calculations of the political elites of Japan in the 1860s, Prussia in the early nineteenth century and Russia in the mid-nineteenth and the early twentieth century.

The industrialisation and democratisation of warfare meant that both the division between war and peace on the one hand, and military and non-military activities on the other, became blurred: the pace of modern warfare meant that peace became increasingly a period of war preparation. Nations would win or lose wars according to the adequacy of their preparations before the outbreak of war. By the Second World War, international conflict had become a struggle between whole peoples, not just of specialised military organisations. This was reflected in the formation of extensive military-industrial complexes, and the batteries of state regulatory powers over the economy and society.

A fourth effect of war upon the nature of the modern nation-state has been the way in which the bureaucratic state machine that was created primarily for prosecuting war was turned instead to the task of resolving some of the problems relating to the social rights of citizenship and welfare in time of peace, and generally to the task of socio-economic management.

War and the Nation-State: the way ahead

In Western nation-states a substantial restructuring of military power has occurred since 1945 – what military sociologists in the 1970s such as Janowitz and Van Doorn referred to as the decline of mass armed forces and the emergence instead of a force-in-being. As James Burk has argued, these two types of military organisation may be contrasted in terms of three dimensions: their mission, their force structure, and the question of citizenship service.[7] The primary goal of the mass armed force is to achieve military victory wherever it is deployed. The mission of the force-in-being, on the other hand, is not so straightforward. Of course no armed force deliberately seeks to fail in achieving its objectives. However, in this case the main goal is to deter the outbreak of international conflict in the first place and then to limit its scope should conflict nevertheless occur. Indecisive outcomes are acceptable if that is the price to be paid for a political settlement.

In terms of force structure, the mission of war-winning leads mass armed forces to build numerically large forces in wartime, as the relatively simple division of labour dependent on rifle infantrymen – parallelling the mass production work force in the civilian economy – allows for a reliance on non-professionals conscripted in time of war and demobilised in time of peace. A relatively small professional cadre remains on active duty for war preparation and to train conscripts.

In contrast, for the force-in-being, the mission of peacekeeping, or of achieving some military objective short of outright victory, requires it to be permanently mobilised, while its dependence on technologically sophisticated weapons of mass destruction means that the military division of labour is much more complex. Consequently, greater emphasis is placed on longer service professionals instead of short-term conscripts. Even if the formal system of conscription is retained it is diluted in the direction of professionalism. Thus in Europe over the 25 years between 1961 and 1986 the average number of months which conscripts had to serve decreased from a minimum of 18 months to one of 12. The size of the force-in-being is moderate, and while larger than the mass armed force in time of peace, it is considerably smaller than the mass armed force at war. By being permanently mobilised there are relatively small fluctuations in the force-in-being over time.[8]

There have been three main causes of this broad shift in the social structure of military power: first, modern weapon technologies require skill levels which limit the usefulness of short-term conscripts. Furthermore, in the nuclear age the destructive power of modern arsenals, in addition to their expense, means that it is difficult to retain war-winning as the defining mission of armed forces. Deterrence places constraints upon the goals of military organisations.

Secondly, shifts in international relations since 1945, and particularly the collapse of the colonial empires of Britain, France and Belgium, altered the military requirements of these states' armed forces. The growth of Third World nationalism and the establishment of numerous new nation-states limited the utility of force in serving the political aims of ex-colonial powers, while the cold war focused military efforts on the development of a force-in-being to face the Soviet threat.

The third cause of the decline of mass armed force is socio-cultural change: specifically post-Second World War affluence and a reluctance to forgo the benefits of consumerism for military service; a more individualistic climate and changing attitudes towards authority; and a reluctance to express a commitment to the national state through military service.

The end of the cold war, a main foundation of the force-in-being, heralds further changes in the social organisation of military power.

Before we analyse such changes, however, this geopolitical development should be placed in the broader context of other fundamental social changes in these 'new times' of ours. Our 'new times' are defined by a number of related social processes.[9] The first is globalisation: the growth of an interdependent, world economic system co-ordinated through transnational corporations and a range of other international and transnational organisations, the operations of which have been facilitated by the electronic revolution in the means of communication. Secondly, and connected with globalisation, our times are characterised by processes of regionalisation and transregionalisation. That is to say, while the regional differentiation between 'core' and 'peripheral' areas is hardly new in economic history, it *is* novel in that overlapping regional specialisations develop along quite different dimensions. Complex hierarchies of regional specialisations develop in which relations of economic superiority may be quite out of kilter with relations of military superiority. At the same time, the global economy means that strategies of autarky are ruled out and transregional co-ordination becomes mandatory for those responsible for managing economic development. Thirdly, in the context of the global system, the number and types of international actor are increasing: sovereign states are now joined by transnational corporations and other international and transnational actors, including emergent politico-economic blocs such as the 'big three' of America, Japan and the European Community. Fourthly, I refer the increasing impact of international law on the conduct of states, as may be observed when one examines the role, for example, of the European Community or of the International Court of Human Rights.

Finally, and as something of a counter-reaction to the growing impact of transnational and international organisations on the global political system, our times have witnessed the development of nationalist and regional/separatist movements which articulate demands for political autonomy and independence. In part, these may be viewed as nationalisms of frustration against the larger political and economic processes outlined above. The much-vaunted decline of the nation-state thus depends upon one's vantage point: whether looking outwards from the big three blocs, or looking hungrily into them from the less economically privileged parts of the globe.

What are the consequences of these processes for the modern, developed nation-state? Let me point to three.

First, as David Held as suggested recently, it can be argued that relations of economic, political and cultural interdependence across the globe are undermining the sovereignty – the legal/constitutional independence to make decisions – as well as the autonomy – the effective power to implement decisions – of nation-states in regard to all aspects of their security. On this argument, their sovereignty and autonomy in relation to economic, social, politico-military and even ecological security are all diminished. Of course, relations of global interdependence have been characteristic of the emerging capitalist world system since the sixteenth century. But today globalisation has reached a qualitatively new stage because of its linkage with the other social and political processes outlined earlier.[10]

For Held, the consequences for nation-states, including new states thrown up by the processes of globalisation, is that their operation in an

> ever more complex international system both limits their autonomy and infringes ever more upon their sovereignty. Any conception of sovereignty which interprets it as an illimitable form of public power is undermined. Sovereignty itself has to be conceived today as already divided among a number of agencies national, international and transnational and limited by the very nature of this plurality.[11]

The second consequence of these new times for the nation-state is that processes related to globalisation are not politically neutral but linked to the spread of liberal capitalism and its likely global hegemony. This, indeed, is the basis of Fukuyama's 'end of history' thesis. In so far as this occurs, then as liberal theorists have been right to stress, war and military power will decline as mechanisms of resolving disputes amongst liberal capitalist societies. They will increasingly be confined to the interface between the capitalist and the non-capitalist world.

This interface will no longer be structured by a bipolar superpower conflict and will develop in a context where the Communist road to modernity has lost legitimacy. This opens up the prospect not only for the advances of liberal democracy but also for conflicts amongst regional powers, as predator nations try to take advantage of the interregnum between a bipolar world and, perhaps, a global international political system with collective security via the United Nations and underpinned by the military might of the one remaining superpower. While war and military power will be confined to the interface between the capitalist and the non-capitalist world, it is certainly questionable whether it will be easy for the developing world to tread the road to liberal democracy. As Weber and Tocqueville warned, democracy has a liberal and an authoritarian face, and perhaps the latter is the one most often shown. We may well see this occurring in the newly enfranchised states of eastern Europe. In any case, the question must arise – especially concerning the relations between the liberal capitalist and the non-liberal capitalist world, and particularly those parts of which control scarce resources crucial for the survival of industrial societies – to what extent the end of the cold war has prefaced the opening of a new and troublesome era of conflicts between North and South, as the advanced industrial societies seek to preserve their security through military means.

These developments provide the setting in which one can address the third consequence of these 'new times'. This concerns the organisation of the military power of the modern Western nation-state. Here one can perceive a third phase in the social organisation of military power: what Charles Moskos has identified as a shift from a force-in-being to a cadre reserve system as part of the development of what he calls a warless society.[12] The Gulf War has proved merely to be a short-term hiccup in the deeper process of downsizing and restructuring military forces. Moskos is not predicting a world without war; rather he is suggesting that war 'at least between superpowers and major European powers is no longer the principal, much less inevitable mode of conflict resolution'.[13] However, Moskos is fairly sanguine about the persistence of regional conflicts and internal wars within countries along with the ethnic strife often connected with great population movements, and the likelihood that the major powers will be drawn into these situations.

In this developing social and political context, Moskos predicts the following profile for the armed forces. Given longer warning times, the active duty force will shrink dramatically to a well-paid, professional cadre which would train less well compensated, long-term reservists. A militia and territorial defence system will evolve. The management technician will be supplemented by the soldier/scholar as the officer corps becomes part of the general advisory service to the state on matters of international security. Thus education and expertise in security studies, broadly defined, will become more important than a narrow focus on war-fighting, strategy and tactics. At the same time, in so far as states persist with the practice of conscription, civilian service will become a common alternative to service in the armed forces. These developments will be associated with a blurring of the division between the different components of the national security system. As Martin Edmonds has argued, internal regional and ethnic strife has already undermined the traditional military/police divide in many states.[14] Moskos argues that this process will continue as armed forces take on not only more policing functions but also non-military tasks such as civilian disaster management. Moskos also contends that the public will become more sceptical about the armed forces and that, consequently, their social status will undergo a process of relative decline. Furthermore, the services will increasingly have their work cut out to preserve their share of public expenditure against the competing claims of the ecological or environmental lobby, health, transport and other areas with greater legitimacy in public perceptions. The question arises that, while such a modern armed force might be appropriate for demilitarised liberal societies, how would it fare (even as part of a multilateral and even multinational force) against non-liberal regimes with substantial military assets? Armed forces that are tailored specifically to perform tasks short of all-out war may find themselves unbalanced and ill-equipped to engage in the more traditional military tasks, should the need ever again arise.

Conclusion

The trend towards what has been termed a cadre/reserve system as part of a warless society seems to me to be a fruitful hypothesis when looking at the current prospects for Western armed forces, or indeed of the armed forces of any capitalist, liberal democracy. However, we must be careful not to become entrapped in evolutionary or 'unfolding' models of contemporary history. Moskos accepts that his thesis on the social organisation of military power hinges on a decline in the prospect of war as a means of resolving conflicts amongst capitalist, liberal democracies and the implicit claim that interventions by these powers in so-called Third World disputes can be disentangled from serious confrontations amongst major powers and/or the superpowers themselves. Furthermore, it seems to me that his case also rests on the implicit assumption that, in so far as armed forces do become involved in this way, then the conflicts would essentially be 'small wars' rather as in the colonial past and in the more recent 'brushfire war' era. Let us assume for a moment a continuing trend towards liberal global capitalism in which the path of 'reform' in the states of the former Soviet Union and a shift from dictatorship to democracy in the Middle East following the Gulf War are seen as positive indicators and as steps towards the realisation of a system of collective security centred on the United Nations. If so, one can envisage further changes in the social organisation of military power, and in particular, the development of multinational forces, that is to say, an extension of the sort of arrangement discussed in the context of the possible emergence of a pan-European security system.

But what if the spread of capitalist liberal democracy does not take place as envisaged in this manner? What if, from the standpoint of the developed world, we are facing a scenario of wars with major regional 'have-not' powers? What if the Gulf War proved not to be a one-off event? In regard to these threats, the difficulties of developing genuinely multinational – and not just multilateral – forces as an arm of the UN will be lessened somewhat by the end of the cold war and the prospect of a system of collective security underwritten by the United States. This would be a Pax Americana to mediate security between the developed and the developing world. The only super-power left could play this role, but only in so far as the relatively non-militarised major economic powers such as Germany and Japan are prepared to underwrite it economically. However, while the threats to capitalist democracy from regional dictatorships may well persist (after all, with the industrialisation of war it is not so difficult for middling economic powers to acquire the military means of becom-ing a serious regional military threat) so too will serious divisions amongst the major capitalist powers themselves. As Will Hutton has suggested recently with regard to conflicts over GATT and agricul-ture, let alone in the case of the Gulf War, we could easily witness a fairly rapid shift from a bipolar, through a short-lived unipolar world – with a weak USA at the top, to a 'multipolar world of competing trade, currency and security blocs'.[15] While those conflicts might be insufficient to provide the basis of a *casus belli* between the capitalist powers, it is not unreasonable to suppose that an unwillingness to trust the guarantees of the United States or, of course, a reluctance on its part to give them, might provoke one or more blocs into the rational response of establishing their own revised, military security systems adequate to meet the prospect of changing regional security threats. At the same time, it also seems reasonable to suppose that in this global age such arrangements would not be developed and applied in isolation from the United Nations. The extent to which these emergent security systems were based on not just multilateral but multinational forces and structured along the lines of a cadre/ reserve model, would reveal the degree to which the social structure of military power had managed to transcend the nation-state. Given the persistence of the machiavellian factor of the pursuit of power, however, this social development would still fall well short of the global security systems promised by the utopian, progressive models of social change which we have inherited from nineteenth century social theory.

8

International Lawyers and Security in the 1990s

Glen Plant

Many older practising English lawyers, upon being introduced to an international lawyer will offer the stock reaction, based upon a dimly-recollected reading of the traditional textbook on jurisprudence, Salmon on Jurisprudence: 'Public international law. Ah yes', they will say, 'Isn't the point about it that it really isn't law at all?' And I have a stock answer to that: 'Regardless of the technicalities, like the absence of a central legislature to prescribe international laws and a central executive or binding judicial system to enforce them', I respond, 'states, like people, do not in general like to be seen breaking the law. Even Hitler sought legal excuses before he invaded innocent countries. Even if it is frequently reliant for its effectiveness on self-control and community pressure, international law is still law, and most states will take it into account, not as some academic check-list, but as an integral part of their policy-making, including policy-making in crisis situations.'

So there are a good many international lawyers around, and the law concerning the use of force and international peace and security is a major part of their stock-in-trade. Nevertheless, opportunities to practice are limited, so that most are academic lawyers. The practice of international law is largely limited to employment in bureaucratic posts with inter-governmental organisations and foreign offices, and only the most eminent academics and retired bureaucratic international lawyers traditionally have private practices – in Britain at the bar, but increasingly in the leading solicitors' firms also.

In order to appreciate how lawyers look at security problems for the future, therefore, it is important to have some insight into the roles traditionally played, and likely to be played during the 1990s, by the various sorts of international lawyer in times of international conflict.

Two cases in particular are worth analyzing here: the crisis leading up to the outbreak of the 1991 Gulf War, where legal advice seems to have been properly assimilated by British decision-makers, and the

92

Suez crisis of 1956, where it was not. The Suez example serves to show what is *not* likely to happen in the 1990s.

We should not assume that international lawyers can normally claim to be major influences on the formation of policy. In a country such as Britain in particular, where the lawyer's role is traditionally seen as that of a professional, independent expert to be consulted as occasion arises, rather than as an integral part of the decision-making process (as in the USA), international lawyers are quick to disclaim any such role, at least below the ranks of senior legal advisers. Nevertheless, they are a force for stability and continuity in the formation of policy and in a sense constitute a racial memory and even, perhaps, the 'conscience' of policy-making and military commands, since they can not only point to precedents but can also point out the full consequences of creating an unfortunate precedent for the future, which might be unscrupulously exploited by others less respectful of legal constraints. They can best do this by pointing policy-makers or military commanders towards a particular one of a number of alternative courses of action, or even suggesting an alternative themselves which the policy-makers have not considered.

It cannot be said that international lawyers as a species are over-paid, so for that reason it is unfair to extend to them some of the unpopularity of lawyers in general. Nevertheless, it is only natural for policy-makers and military commanders to be impatient of the sort of international lawyer who says 'No, you cannot do that. It is illegal'. A popular lawyer is one who explains how something can be done. But there are times when the international lawyer must properly say 'No'.

When Anthony Eden called a small meeting of ministers on 16 October 1956 to discuss the plan to intervene in Suez following Nasser's nationalisation of the canal, his response to the suggestion that the Foreign Office Legal Adviser be brought in on the matter was, in effect, 'the lawyers are always against our doing anything. For God's sake, keep them out of it. This is a political affair'. He thus acted later that month without even a reasonable legal argument for intervention in place, let alone a cast-iron case. He appears to have taken his advice from Lord Kilmuir (the then Lord Chancellor, who was not an experienced international lawyer, and, although a member of the Cabinet, was entitled to advise only in a private capacity) rather than from the government's official legal advisers, the Law Officers and the Foreign Office Legal Adviser. The official advisers all consistently insisted that intervention would be illegal in the circumstances then prevailing.

The result was disaster. Britain and France were forced out of Suez with their tails between their legs. The resignations of the Law Officers, the Attorney-General and Solicitor-General, were avoided only by adopting a policy of justifying the intervention purely on policy grounds while avoiding all mention of the legal aspects. The Foreign Office legal advisers were left very concerned that they would be obliged to explain to their foreign colleagues that the decision to intervene was taken without their advice.

Fortunately, that was an almost unique error. Legal advice was, I believe, properly taken by the British government from the proper quarters during the Gulf crisis of 1990–91. Nevertheless, the incident serves to illustrate that the taking of sound, international, legal advice is essential in the modern sphere of the use of force. The age of thoughtless gunboat diplomacy is long over. One of the really note-worthy facets of the Gulf crisis, indeed, was that the USA and Britain were at great pains from August 1990 to keep the United Nations 'on side' and to emphasise the degree to which they were trying to avoid civilian casualties during bombing raids carried out after the 15 January deadline for Iraq to withdraw from Kuwait. This was not just good policy; it was good law too.

The United Nations Security Structure

The post-Second World War over international law concerning peace and security is in theory straightforward and in practice quite complex. The Security Council is given, under Chapter VII of the UN Charter, a virtual monopoly over the use of force to defeat aggression. States, alone or collectively with their allies, are entitled to use force only in self-defence as a *temporary* measure until the Security Council starts to take effective measures. The Security Council's forces were supposed to be provided by individual member states by agreements made under Article 43 of the Charter.

Because of the cold war, however, the Security Council had never, until 1990, worked in the manner envisaged. No forces were ever made available to it under Article 43 and, with two or three anomalous exceptions, it never really exercised Chapter VII powers. As a result, wars have gone largely unchecked, and the right to self-defence has tended to be abused or turned into a *permanent* right. The Gulf crisis was, however, apart from the absence of agreements under Article 43, in my view almost a textbook application of Chapter VII. The first of the 12 Security Council resolutions, Resolution 660 of 2 August 1990, determined the existence of a breach of the peace under Article 39 and thus triggered the possibility of movement on to and up the ladder of 'enforcement action' measures which the Council is able to take under the several substantive articles of Chapter VII. The embargo against Iraq set up by Resolution 661 of 6 August 1990 represented the first step up this ladder, invoking measures not involving the use of armed forces. When these sanctions came to be considered as unlikely to work (at least within a reasonable period of time), Resolution 678 was passed on 29 November 1990, permitting 'Member States co-operating with the Government of Kuwait' – if Iraq did not withdraw from Kuwait by 15 January 1991 – to 'use all necessary means to uphold and implement Security Council Resolution 660 (1990) and all subsequent resolutions and to restore international peace and security in the area'. It can be argued that the subsequent military action was action in collective self-defence by certain member states, and not Article 42 action, as the latter would not arguably be permissible, except through the use of Article 43-type forces. But the better view, in my opinion, is that Resolution 678 escalated the Security Council's actions up the ladder so as to authorise the use of forceful measures under Ch VII though not specifically under Article 42 itself. The much-debated words 'all appropriate measures' clearly permit the use of armed force.

There is likely to be increased potential for armed conflict in the 1990s, as countries such as the former USSR and Yugoslavia suffer complete disintegration, and new development and environmental pressures bite harder. It is difficult to predict what form these conflicts will take and whether external powers will be involved in opposing local acts of aggression and in restoring peace and security under the auspices of the Security Council acting under Chapter VII, or whether such a scenario will fail to emerge because of a renewed use of the veto by, in particular, Russia or China.

What is certain is that wars will continue to be fought and international lawyers somewhere are likely to be called upon for their views on each occasion.

The Role of International Lawyers

So who are the major actors in a possible future crisis from the legal point of view? There are perhaps four types of international lawyer with a role to play: (1) Government legal advisers; (2) the legal advisers in relevant global and regional inter-governmental organisations and in the International Committee of the Red Cross (ICRC); (3) academic lawyers; and (4) the military themselves, both lawyers and non-lawyers. The last category should not be a surprise. There is no person more directly involved in the application of pure international law than the soldier, sailor or airman, and especially senior officers. The military must frequently make decisions on the spot which involve questions of international law, and it is for this reason, for example, that the Geneva Conventions emphasise the need to disseminate knowledge of their contents, and this most especially among members of the armed forces.

Easily the most important category of these four is, and is likely to remain, that of government legal advisers, and I shall dwell on them for some time.

Government Legal Advisers

A comprehensive analysis of the role of government legal advisers in the Gulf crisis would involve at the very least an account of the legal governmental structures of each of the 15 serving members of the Security Council during 1990, when the 12 relevant Resolutions were passed. The periods of service of five of the elected members did, of course, lapse on 1 January 1991 and they were replaced by five new members. Any analysis should probably also extend to the other major actors too, namely other states besides Security Council members co-operating militarily with Kuwait, as well as Israel, Jordan and Iran. A proper analysis would also seek to look at the degree of each country's adherence to legal advice. Nevertheless, for our present analytical purposes it would be sensible to concentrate on the two most active members of the anti-Iraq alliance, the USA and Britain.

It is axiomatic to point out, however, that every country organises its legal advice differently. Ex-British colonies tend to follow the British pattern of centralising international legal advice in the Attorney-General's Office and/or the Foreign and Commonwealth Office (FCO). Others distribute it among legal departments in a number of ministries. Many countries rely exclusively on bureaucratic advice, whereas others draw on academic expertise too. Many countries have in-house permanent legal advisers in their foreign services, while others transfer legally qualified diplomats freely between their legal and non-legal departments and have no or only a few permanent lawyers. All countries' equivalents of Ministers of Justice (in Britain perhaps the Lord Chancellor) and Attorneys- and Solicitors-General are political appointments; but some countries extend the practice of political appointment to their senior foreign office legal advisers too, whereas most such appointments are in-house. Some states have unusual arrangements. In Colombia, a member of the Security Council in 1990, an attempt to render international legal advice bipartisan is made by consulting an advisory council on foreign affairs made up of appointees of both the Congress and the President. Each system has its advantages and disadvantages.

In Britain it is clear that, despite the Suez precedent, the Lord

Chancellor is not the proper source of legal advice. He does not serve in the Cabinet as its legal adviser, although his views will, of course, carry great weight. Rather he is a member of the Cabinet, because he is the head of the Judiciary, presiding officer of the House of Lords and Head of the Lord Chancellor's Department. In any event, he will not normally be an expert in international law.

The senior legal advisers on international law are the Attorney-General and, below him, the Solicitor-General. The '30 year rule' applies to their work in this area, and there is thus no specific evidence in the public domain that their views were sought during the Gulf crisis of 1990–91, but I have no doubt that they were on the most difficult and important questions of law, such as the US-British-Australian decision unilaterally to enforce the UN Maritime embargo in mid-August 1990. Indeed, there is also a Foreign and Commonwealth Office legal adviser seconded to their staff to act as the link with the FCO legal advisers, who are responsible for all international legal questions not of sufficient importance to go to the Law Officers.

The FCO has a small corps of full-time legal advisers (at present about 24). The Legal Adviser himself has overall responsibility for advice and below him the next three most senior advisers exercise a supervisory role over particular sectors of the Legal Adviser's work. But, rather like a barrister in a set of chambers, each legal adviser, however junior, has his own functional, geographic and administrative departments to advise. Promotion depends on 'dead men's shoes', except in regard to the post of Legal Adviser itself, and the career structure this presents is not very dynamic. The Kuwait crisis of August 1990 fell within the remit of the third most senior legal adviser, who was advising the Middle East Department (MED) of the FCO, which is, it need not be explained, a department which is likely to be allocated to a senior adviser.

The British system has the virtue that the legal adviser in question will have had the opportunity to cover during a career of 20 or more years most of the relevant areas of international law, and will have been in an adviser-client relationship with many of the relevant policy-makers already. He will also have served as British legal adviser on two or three three-year foreign postings, possibly one at the UN, and so will understand intimately the workings of the Security Council. The disadvantage relative to, for example, his counterpart in Canada (which also served on the Security Council during the Gulf crisis), where most legal advisers are not full-time, is that he will not have intimate experience of policy-formulation to anything like the same degree, so that there may be some intellectual divide between him and his policy-making colleagues, and his advice is therefore in danger of being that much less practical in the light of political realities.

One peculiarly British problem is the small number of legal advisers to deal with the international legal problems of a country which has extensive international interests. The number of legal advisers has hardly expanded at all since the 1960s, and the sheer volume of work is a real problem. By way of contrast, the USA has about 150 such advisers to deal with a not wholly disproportionate volume of work. One thing is clear, however. After the Suez *débâcle*, the legal advisers' advice is sought, not only by the diplomats in the MED and other interested FCO departments, but also by Ministers. The legal adviser and departmental representatives will have met FCO ministers frequently during the Gulf crisis.

Legal advice in the USA, by contract, is more of a political game than it is in Britain. First, there is no guarantee that it will come from the Attorney-General's Office or the Department of State (DOS) legal advisers alone (or indeed at all). There are several international lawyers in the National Security Council and in the Department of Defence and, indeed, Dick Cheney, the Secretary of State for Defense in 1990–91, was himself an international lawyer of some renown. He was intimately involved in the efforts to seek a peaceful solution before hostilities started. For example, in discussing with the Iraqis a bargain involving their withdrawal from Kuwait followed by arbitration over their claims to the Bubiyan, Warba and associated islands, and the Rumaliya oil field. It seems that Iraq would have had a reasonable chance of success in the latter, and, in my opinion, was being offered an advantageous arrangement at the time.

Second, within the DOS the Legal Adviser's office has to fight for its own political turf. In the USA, lawyers move much more easily between government, academe and law practice than their counterparts in Britain, The new legal adviser, in 1991, Edwin Williamson, was a corporate lawyer with a leading New York law firm, Sullivan and Cromwell, specialising in securities law before his appointment. He is not primarily an international lawyer, and Secretary of State Baker, himself a lawyer, could well seek legal advice elsewhere, for example, from one of the other talented lawyers whom he appointed to top political posts, such as Bob Kimmit (Head of Political Affairs and Baker's number three), who formerly worked for the US Treasury and then practised in the prominent Washington firm, Sidley and Austin.

DOS legal advisers may thus well have been by-passed partly or completely on this and other recent occasions of the use of force, such as the American interventions in Grenada and Panama. There are many talented DOS legal advisers, but there is no guarantee that their advice will be adopted even by their own heads of department, let alone exert any influence beyond them. The Americans also make more use of academic lawyers than do the British. This practice is not as institutionalised as in some countries, such as Germany, where a panel of three senior academics is consulted by the Federal Foreign Office on important questions of international law. But there is always at least one academic seconded to the DOS advisers, invariably chosen by the Legal Adviser himself, who thus might exert a disproportionate influence. There is also some frustration among the staff that some senior legal posts are political appointments not open to career staff. Finally, the DOS has long employed three legal advisers to take care of legal advice to its own UN Mission on a more or less permanent basis, so that there is little opportunity for individual legal advisers in Washington to gather direct experience of the workings of the UN.

Degree of Divergence of International Legal Advice

It follows that, whatever the convergence of policy attitudes of Britain and the USA may have been in the Gulf crisis, the surrounding legal advice will not necessarily have been the same. Thus when the USA, Britain and Australia moved unilaterally to enforce the Maritime embargo established by Resolution 661 in mid-August 1990, the USA relied solely on its alleged right to do so in self-defence and used the term 'interdiction', which recalled President Kennedy's language upon his imposition of the Cuban quarantine in October 1962. Britain has never, to my knowledge, accepted the legality that the Cuban quarantine could be based on the right of self-defence, and in the Gulf case was careful to say that the 'naval enforcement measures', as it preferred to call them, were only lawful because of the combination of three factors, each insufficient in itself: the right of self-defence; the existence of Resolutions 660 and 661; and a specific invitation to enforce the embargo from the Emir of Kuwait.

Nevertheless, there is always likely to be a large degree of convergence of political/bureaucratic legal advice given to allies as close as Britain and the USA. A politically-appointed lawyer's advice will generally tend to be centred around his perception of the political advantage to himself. A bureaucratic lawyer is likely to be affected, at least subconsciously, by the realities of bureaucratic life. Ministers and senior policy-making colleagues will expect answers which allow them to perform predetermined policies, and these policies will generally have been formed in combination with allied governments. In addition, a bureaucrat cannot be seen to make any mistakes in high-profile work, almost regardless of the cost or loss of efficiency in low-profile work. All of these factors are likely to influence the form and content of legal advice and to tend towards uniformity of advice among allies.

Legal advice in the Gulf crisis covered a multitude of matters besides those already mentioned. They included: the legality of Kuwait's absorption into Iraq; the competence of the Security Council to clarify the meaning of its resolutions and so to determine which foodstuffs could be let through 'in humanitarian circumstances' under the embargo resolutions; breaches of the Vienna Conventions on Diplomatic and Consular Relations; the extension of the embargo to aircraft and the use of ICAO-approved interception procedures; breaches of the Fourth Geneva Convention and other human rights instruments by Iraq concerning the treatment of civilians; the questions of possible reparations from Iraq and the possible prosecution of senior Iraqis for war crimes; breaches of the Third Geneva Convention and the role of the ICRC; whether or not Article 42 of the Charter permits the use of force on the basis of Resolution 678; and the scope of allied war aims.

One refreshing observation is that most of the questions, apart from those of the unilateral enforcement of the embargo and the scope of the war aims were relatively straightforward in legal terms. It follows that, despite the evidence of grounds for diversity, in practice the legal attitudes of the majority of the members of the Security Council, and, most importantly, of the USA and Britain remained quite similar. Nevertheless, international lawyers should ask themselves whether or not, given the unprecedented success of the sanctions between August and the end of November, their legal advice was an insufficient brake upon the political impetus towards the use of force.

Any situation can also change. The key words in one of the most important Resolutions passed during the Gulf crisis (number 678) were: 'and to restore international peace and security in the area'. Soviet and Chinese support in the Security Council was essential to the continued prosecution of an unchanged mandate. But the two countries questioned whether allied actions exceeded that mandate. Given the change in 1991 in the constitution of the Security Council to include countries such as India, which was concerned that the allies might be exceeding their mandate, it was clear that the allies had to work hard to maintain the commitment to Resolution 678 as it existed in 1990.

And what of legal advisers in the 1990s? It remains to be seen what form international conflicts will take and what the UN's role will be. If the UN takes on a new lease of life, the advice given during 1990–91 may well serve as a model for future cases. Otherwise it will be business as usual, applying a mixture of the law of self-defence and analogies with the pre-Charter laws of war. My guess is that the

UN will not repeat this kind of enforcement action, except when major world resources are under threat, as in the Iraqi crisis of the early 1990s.

Legal Advisers to International Organisations

Legal advisers to international organisations are servants of the organisations and so supply legal advice on a continuing basis to the chief executives of them, in the UN's case the Secretary-General, and will provide legal opinions on aspects of law within each secretariat's competence, such as UN procedural law, if requested to do so by member states. The main global organisations involved in the Gulf crisis were the UN, the World Bank and the ICAO. There is no evidence of their legal advisers being asked to prepare any legal opinions, but they will have kept their directors fully briefed. The same is true of a large number of regional organisations.

Finally, the lawyers of the ICRC, which is essentially a Swiss body, endeavoured to find ways to persuade Iraq to comply with its obligations under the Geneva Conventions, in particular its obligation, in the absence of a Protecting Power, to allow the ICRC to act as such a 'Protecting Power' and, for example, to visit prisoners of war. But, as always, it comes down entirely to reliance upon persuasion and, at most, the sort of (non-finger-pointing) public appeals it made during the Iraq–Iran war of the 1980s. Iraq took a totally illegal attitude in connecting the question of civilian bombing casualties with the question of ICRC visits to allied prisoners of war. The ICRC could do nothing except work to persuade Iraq to change its mind.

Academic International Lawyers

In the context of this analysis, academic international lawyers should be read to mean those at the top of their profession, who are also invariably those in private practice. This category of lawyer, whose opinions can be regarded as a subsidiary source of international law itself, tends to be concentrated in the USA and the UK, with perhaps half a dozen in each. They have an impact on policy-making in a number of ways. Firstly they write the leading textbooks and articles, which a harassed legal adviser will rely heavily upon. The Lord Chancellor relied heavily on a passage in *Oppenheim on International Law* (the international lawyers' bible) in 1956, and apparently misinterpreted it. He also relied upon a passage in an article written by C.H.M. Waldock, then Chichele Professor of International Law at Oxford, although there is no evidence that he approached him in person to check the correctness of his interpretation. Having said this, however, it should be noted that in government and international organisations legal advisers also make substantial contributions to international legal literature in their spare time. Indeed, the FCO Legal Adviser between 1987 and 1991, Sir Arthur Watts, has been preparing with Sir Robert Jennings, President of the World Court and formerly Whewell Professor of International Law at Canbridge, a new edition of *Oppenheim on International Law.*

Secondly, on a more interventionist note, leading international lawyers may also warn the relevant legal advisers of their views that errors are being made. They may be invited by the legal advisers to give their views or may do so on their own initiative, in person, by private letter or through the media. In 1956 Robert (now Sir Robert) Jennings and Lord McNair, a retired, eminent international lawyer wrote to *The Times* over Suez.

Finally, they may be instructed to give expert advice or to appear in court as counsel.

Even the lesser mortals among international lawyers have a role. They may indicate ways in which the law should be applied when government policy is clearly not taking nor intending to take the point on board.

A legal matter of great importance which arose from the 1991 Gulf War was that of deliberate and 'collateral' environment damage by belligerents. This issue gives rise to questions of state responsibility and personal criminal liability of the perpetrators under international law, which in the past did not normally arise in situations of international armed conflict. But deliberate environmental damage may well become a regular feature of future wars.[1]

Members of the Armed Forces

The importance of members of the armed forces being conversant with the Geneva Conventions needs no repetition. One factor present in 'normal' conflict situations which is little thought of is the self-interest of a country in ensuring that its own troops comply with the humanitarian law of war, not only out of self-interest alone but also simply so as not to undermine their own morale. The Iran–Iraq War and the Gulf War at least on one side, seemed to represent a return to barbaric methods of conducting warfare. In 1986 the ICRC adopted a resolution noting 'a disturbing decline in respect for international humanitarian law . . .' I hope, as an international lawyer, that this trend does not continue and that the humanitarian law of war, as well as the UN Charter, will come out of this turbulent period of conflict strengthened rather than weakened.

Security in the 1990s and Beyond

Michael Nicholson

Conflict studies, conflict research and conflict analysis, terms which are used more or less interchangeably, comprise an ill-defined discipline. Those who call themselves 'conflict researchers' are very diverse and include such people as John Burton, Brian Crozier and Anatol Rapoport, men who would not only disagree with each other but barely understand what the others are talking about. Their one centre of interest is conflict – but this applies to everyone else who is interested in international relations, strategy, war studies or whatever. Thus one is led into the supposition that 'conflict analyst' is the term given to anyone interested in conflict who does not readily fit into any of the more conventionally recognised categories – the set of people who are not otherwise members of a set, or the set of isolates. I readily fit into such a set.

As my set membership is vague and more or less meaningless, I had better describe my background and approach. I was brought up by the economists, kindly folk for the most part, but apt to have a certain intellectual attitude to things which has been considered, by those less fortunate in their intellectual upbringing, as arrogant – a view, of course, ascribable to envy. My defection from my parent discipline created no crisis within it, though it was reported that one of my former colleagues, though I hope not one of my former friends, had described me sadly, if not entirely accurately, as 'a good man fallen among strategists'. Economics sets a style of thought upon those brought up in the tradition which is hard to replace – even assuming, of course, that it was desirable to replace it. It is similar to being brought up by the Jesuits. Once in the system one is forever within it and one may oppose it but never escape it. An atheist brought up by the Jesuits is forever an atheistical Jesuit, and no doubt any converts to Islam pursue their new faith in a thoroughly Jesuitical manner. Likewise an economist, no matter how far he may roam intellectually, whether into psychoanalysis, literary criticism or Zen Buddhism, does so gently musing on marginal costs and optimisation problems. There is no escape and neither, to be frank, have I really tried to look for one. I think that the economist's approach to some of these matters is largely a healthy one. The serious developments in most fields come from the periphery, not the centre. I believe that the merging of the economists' methods with those of other disciplines such as history and psychology is more likely to produce results in our understanding of international violence than developments which emerge purely from within the discipline of international relations itself.

It is important to begin, therefore, with an understanding of the nature of conflict research followed by one of the nature of security. It is also necessary to consider the normative distinctions between the various disciplines which pertain to security, such as conflict research, strategy, international relations and peace studies, and finally to consider some problems for the future and how we should approach them, particularly in conflict research.

The Nature of Conflict Analysis

Conflict analysis is a discipline characterised by two features. First, conflict is a generic feature of social life which operates at all social levels. This is scarcely a novel remark but I go further. Some at least of the general principles which apply to conflict at one social level apply at others – or so at least we may fruitfully hypothesise. Thus we may consider an activity such as bargaining, which may be carried out between states, between individuals, between management and unions and so on, and believe that we are talking about much the same thing in all cases. The activity of bargaining has similarities in all these settings and we might hope for a general theory of bargaining which covers all its manifestations, though allowing for idiosyncracies in each form or, indeed, in each individual instance. Similarly we may have alliances of states and alliances of individual people or alliances of practically anything, and to cover them all we may have a general theory of alliances. There is a common activity of alliance formation and existence which can apply at all social levels.

The second feature of conflict analysis is that of method: conflict behaviour may be analysed as a social science. By this I mean that we are searching for regularities and generalisations in social behaviour and making theoretical statements which are testable against the evidence. In the philosophy of social science to which I adhere, to the disapproval of at least some analysts I know, I am doubtful of the meaning of a supposed theoretical statement which cannot be tested at least in principle, either directly or indirectly. Thus in considering the proposition that arms races are predisposing factors to war, Michael Wallace considered those arms races and wars since 1816 as found in the mammoth 'Correlates of War' project. This project was a huge data-collection enterprise carried out by David Singer and Melvin Small on data on the international system since the Napoleonic Wars.[1] He found that they were related. Subsequent controversies have been between the statisticians, all taking it for granted that it was data of this sort which were relevant. Another study, done by L.F. Richardson,[2] on whether there were cycles in the onsets of wars, with periods of frequent outbreaks of war and others of fewer, was tested over a similar period on data collected by himself. His analysis showed that there was no such pattern. None of these studies was beyond controversy, but they all show a concern with the questions 'Why do we believe what we believe about the international system? What is relevant evidence for our beliefs?' This is perhaps the core principle behind conflict research – we should be self-conscious about our grounds for belief in generalisations. I emphasise the concern with generalisation. I am not here concerned with the reasons for our belief in particular propositions and am not in any sense in dispute with the historians. I am in dispute with international relations theorists of the classical school, particularly with those of the so-called 'English school', whose failure to grasp the nature of empirical generalisation and the need for testing continues to shock me. It is not sufficient to make such statements as 'the balance of power requires five actors to make it work' and then gesture vaguely towards the nineteenth century as if this one instance justified a generalisation. It requires serious, deductive analysis in terms of a model of the balance of power, along with an analysis of a statistically significant number of instances. If this is impossible, then we are entitled to enquire just what such statements mean. In fact Harrison Wagner's[3] recent work suggests that the number five is false – three is sufficient – though as a cautious modeller he is much more restrained in his claims than the classical school.

Those who become uneasy at the prospect of a battery of correlation coefficients and the like, may be reassured. For all my piety about testing, my aim here is to ask some questions which arise out of this way of thinking, rather than to indulge in that form of thinking itself. In conflict studies we aim to produce a social science patterned on, say, economics, psychology or some parts of sociology. How far this is achievable is an open question. Some critics argue that a social science of this nature – about any form of social behaviour – is impossible, in which case this enterprise falls to the ground along with the other social sciences, and the many purported results (which the sceptics claim are spurious). There is a serious argument for this position. The consequences for academic politics would, of course, be severe if this view were to be seriously accepted. It would involve the closing down of large parts of, amongst other institutions, the London School of Economics. Another criticism is more partial – that while social scientific methods are applicable to economics and psychology and other aspects of social behaviour, conflict analysis, at least in its international form, is somehow special, being perhaps the preserve of gentlemen and not, as other studies, of the rude mechanicals. I have never understood this point of view. If intentional human behaviour in any of its manifestations is amenable to scientific methods then it all should be. I see no justification for some demarcation line around certain parts of it and have yet to read any justification which makes this plausible. Hence we can have conflict analysis *and* the London School of Economics, or neither.

In my urge to be a social scientist there is one final point I should stress. I am anxious to be clear when I am making scientific statements – or indeed any statement about how the world behaves – and when I am making moral statements about how I would like the world to behave. I want to be careful to distinguish between an 'is' and an 'ought' and, much more difficult, to distinguish between an 'is' and a 'wish'. We must be disciplined in trying to keep our categories separate even if we are more or less bound to fail frequently. I am aware of the conceptual problems involved in distinguishing between these categories, but I think that they can be exaggerated, unlike the psychological problems in making such distinctions, which cannot be.

The Nature of Security

Turning now to security, I want to discuss two points: the different forms of security and insecurity on the international scene, and a broader concept of security which goes beyond that traditionally thought of in strategic studies. I begin with international security. First let us assume some inherent hostility between two states. One can increase its security at the expense of the other – that is, it makes the other feel less secure. There are balances where both feel tolerably secure but there is always the possibility that this balance might slip and one increase its security at the expense of the other. In its extreme form this is seen as a zero-sum game, where a constant amount of security has to be distributed between the two states and there is a constant battle for a greater share. However, in less extreme situations it is assumed that there is some distribution of the means of violence such that both states feel more secure than with other distributions. There is also often assumed to be a security dilemma where the persistent search for security in fact leads to a general reduction in security as both increase their capacities. Thus we have a classic case of a non-zero-sum game where there are mutually beneficial outcomes and mutually detrimental ones.

In both these cases the lack of security of the one comes about through the perceived threats of the other. If the perception of threat disappears, however, then both can improve their security and the overall amount of security expands. In general, one would expect this to be a benign, cumulative process, in that once threats began to disappear then more and more would continue to disappear. Indeed, there may well be unilateral acts which increase the security of both parties. In the end the situation is seen as non-conflictual and, the question 'Are we insecure?' ends up by being a non-question. The situation in Western Europe now, as compared with the inter-war years, provides a comparison of the two forms of security. It was perceived as zero-sum in the inter-war years and as not conflictual at all in the military sense in the present era. Some people, of course, would still interpret a non-military situation as essentially conflictual, so it would appear to be still a zero-sum game. Other classic cases of security moving from the zero-sum, to the non-zero-sum, to the non-existent are Canada in relation to the USA and Norway in relation to Sweden. It does happen and is not just the figment of an optimist's imagination. The point is, can it be engineered and encouraged?

This approach fits in with a standard view of state security with the state as the central actor. However, the view that conflict should be analysed at a variety of levels leads psychologically, though not logically, to a greater tendency to speculate on the units of analysis which are dealt with in security studies. In general, security studies concentrate on the security of states or alliances of states. While this might be a useful first approximation, I suggest that this misses the point (though this is a moral view). Security is really a matter of the security of the individual. This might, of course, be loosely related to that of the state, but only loosely. In certain cases the opposite is the case. Let me pose the following definition of the security of an individual. An individual's security is measured by the probability on the day of his or her birth of living to some appropriately advanced age and dying then of 'natural causes'. A secure state is one which contains lots of such people. While life alone is not the only issue and the prospect of a long and healthy life in an antiseptic prison would not properly be regarded as secure in a broader sense, such prisons are relatively rare and I shall assume for convenience that health and liberty are broadly associated. My emphasis is on the security of the individual. Obviously the risks from outside states are an important factor in security in this sense, as we have seen in this decade in the case of wars in the Gulf region, and, unfortunately, in innumerable cases throughout recorded history. Doubtless I have numerous many-times-great grandparents on the east coast of Yorkshire, plying an agricultural trade, whose security was severely impeded by others of my many-times-great grandfathers who were among the more violent immigrants from Denmark. However, this is only one of the threats to security. Internal threats are just as severe. The Iraqis, viewed as a collection of some 16 million people, as distinct from the state of Iraq, have been much more threatened by internal forces over the last decade than external ones. The security of the Roumanian people until 1990 was very poor; but not because there was any particular external threat. In both these cases the threats came from the government. In many cases the threats come from non-governmental groups, as may be seen in Northern Ireland, or indeed from quasi-commercial groups, as in Colombia.

Similar stories can be told of inter-war Europe. This is the era whose lessons re-established realism as a theory of international relations, with E.H. Carr as a prominent teacher of such lessons. In that period internal threats to the security of the individual were as severe as external ones. The gross insecurity of a Spaniard around 1938, for example, arose through the actions of other Spaniards, not because of external threats to the state. The fears of Frenchmen at the same time were as much fears of other Frenchmen who might emulate the Spaniards as of the Germans. The speed with which the Germans did in fact conquer France when the time came was in part owing to the deep divisions in French society then. The security of many Germans themselves, viewed as individuals, was seriously eroded by the internal activities of the Nazi state, particularly if they were Jewish, while many citizens of the Soviet Union of the day lived a life of perpetual and justified terror. The year 1938, a year chosen at random from a number of candidates, was a very insecure time, but only partly because of the expansionism of several of the states of the day, which is the traditionally recognised source of insecurity.

This opens up a range of studies which, on my definition, are central to security studies, but are still inadequately dealt with, unless I have missed even more of the literature I am supposed to be familiar with than I thought. How is it that states become authoritarian and subdue their citizens? When do such states become expansionary and threaten the security of the citizens of other states? In general, what are the conditions for states to adopt patterns of government which threaten their own citizens and those of other lands in manners which we generally find offensive and, at least to some degree, most people in most cultures find offensive?

Moreover, the security of people is affected by many other things than wars, civil wars and repressions. Famines and floods are prominent particularly if one is an inhabitant of a state such as Bangladesh.

Some of the famines are at least partially a consequence of warfare, as in Sudan, but in part they are due to the malice of the environment over which we have little control. We do have secondary control, however, in that, more often than we like to think, apparent acts of God are aggravated by the acts of humans. A.K. Sen's work on famines,[4] where he shows that in many famines the crucial element is the failure of market mechanisms as much as the failure of the crops, is salutary as far as our disclaimers of responsibility are concerned. However, while factors of this sort are clearly crucial if we are to look at the general picture of security as perceived by the victims – and we include such factors as disease to add to the misery count – it is convenient to separate out those problems involving violence from those which do not. It seems to me that there are basically different problems involved in their analysis, and, if we are optimistic, in their alleviation than there are in those which do not, and that these problems involve the deep, dark and sinister mysteries of the human mind to a greater extent than the more conventional treatments of strategic studies (or for that matter conflict analysis) would suggest.

Presuppositions: Normative and Other

It is now appropriate to consider the different sets, if any, of presuppositions which lie behind conflict analysis, strategy, peace studies *et cetera*. These may be conveniently divided into two classes – the normative or moral presuppositions, and the assumptions about human nature. These disciplines are practised by individuals who all have their own particular sets of presuppositions.

First consider the normative presuppositions. Let me recount the tale I tell to my students. People look at the general problems of violence in the international system under four different labels: international relations, conflict analysis, strategy and peace research. In principle, the first two of these are positive disciplines in the sense of describing how the world behaves rather than how it ought to behave. There are normative presuppositions in the sense that the topics chosen for analysis are the consequence of normative principles but the analysis itself is, at least in principle, free from normative judgements. We want simply to know how things work. However, strategy and peace research are overtly based on normative principles: they are 'how to do it' disciplines in which goals are explicitly formulated and the aim of the exercise is to show how to achieve those goals. Strategy, at least as used by students of strategic studies means, if Wolf Mendl and Michael Howard are to be believed, those areas of international behaviour in which force and threats of force are pertinent modes of action. This implies at least two parties, and the strategist is looking at the problem with the interests of one of the parties paramount. This is often the state or an alliance of states but it need not be. Revolutionary strategists such as Mao Tse-tung are looking at the problem from the point of view of the revolutionary group – be it the party, the religion, or whatever, but it is in the context of a violent or potentially violent conflict. This is not to say that strategists are eager to fight – often the contrary – but they still weigh up one group's interests more than the others.

In peace research it is more confused. In principle, peace researchers side with no one (or everyone) and are concerned with the resolution of conflicts with as little violence as possible (and in some versions, none whatsoever), and with a concern for the interests of all parties. However, in some versions, such as that of Galtung and many in the International Peace Research Association, peace research involves an identification with the underprivileged and a positive concern with distributive justice. In this case it becomes a form of strategy, according to my definitions, in that it serves to advance the goals of some people in a conflict situation. The difference, then, in normative values between strategy and peace research becomes an issue of whom you side with.

Nevertheless, conflict analysis in its more socially scientific form has often been thought of as the left-wing approach to international conflict. In its earlier days, in the 1950s, this was probably true. Its principal founder, Lewis Fry Richardson was a Quaker and thus a pacifist, as were some prominent later scholars, such as Kenneth Boulding. Others, such as Anatol Rapoport, deeply distrusted the military of any sort but particularly the American military. Yet others, such as John Burton, whose claims to being a social scientist are tenuous, were under the mistaken impression that social science justified his own left-wing opinions, a view which, if true, would have perhaps lent some credence to Sir Keith (now Lord) Joseph's subsequent view that social science was a left-wing plot. However, I think it was true that the conflict analysts of the fifties and sixties were for the most part politically left of centre and some, such as Galtung, a long way so. However, this is not true today. What 30 years ago would have been called 'conflict studies' is in many places in the United States now called 'international relations' for reasons I shall not go into here (it is often enough discussed elsewhere by myself, among others). The discipline is no longer the preserve of left-wingers but occupied by followers of all political persuasions, as would be expected if my earlier assertion was correct – that the internal nature of the discipline is value-free. I can give an example. One of the most innovative but controversial American scholars in the field is Bruce Bueno de Mesquita. He is a right-wing libertarian conservative. I did not discover this until recently, nor had I suspected it, despite having followed his work carefully over the decade and having written a long critique of some aspects of his work in *The Journal of Conflict Resolution*.[5] My disagreements are substantial but they involved arguments in the theory of games and statistical method. When I wrote them I had no idea of his political position and I still think that our technical differences are totally separate from our equally significant political differences. His work could have been done by a left-winger and my critique could have been made by a right-winger and I suspect, despite our many other disagreements, we would both agree on that.

Now let us turn to the assumptions about human nature which go back to the underlying rift which has divided people along theological, philosophical and practically all other lines ever since we began to speculate. Are humans basically good or bad? In particular, we must deal with the issues of power and violence.

It appears to be the case that, while most people like their own security, many people are not averse to taking away the security of other people. Bertrand Russell,[6] many years ago, in a book which greatly influenced Carr, argued that the impulse to power was a basic human impulse, a view held in a slightly different form by Nietzsche. This approach, in one form or another, underlies the attitudes of many strategists and followers of the realist school of international relations. However, Russell did not relate it exclusively to state power. While I suspect Russell exaggerated the drive for power, he made an important point. Institutions at all social levels, not just the international, need to contain the impulse to power, which so many people, who so manifestly should not hold power, continue to seek and occasionally find. The lust for power is not purely a military phenomenon or even a political one. Nature's bully boys use religious power and economic power, causing damage wherever they go. A weakness in much of the classical realist thinking which lies behind a lot of strategic studies is to identify the urge for power too much with the state and military power. In the last analysis, the urge for power is the urge of individuals for power. In certain cases they may act through the state, but often not. Investigating the internal processes whereby states become authoritarian seems to me a crucial problem. Authoritarianism is not the same as expansionism, but there may be a connection, an empirical proposition which needs to be tested. Thus it seems to be the case that libertarian states rarely fight each other. This is a problem of the search for power which seems to me crucial and without which our general search for an explanation of political violence is inhibited.

Unfortunately we still know little about how to answer such questions. I am tempted to hypothesise that countries such as Iraq under Saddam Hussein, Romania under Ceausescu, the USSR under Stalin, Albania under Hoxha and probably after, are in some ways qualitatively different from the ordinarily authoritarian such as post-Stalin USSR, most of eastern Europe in the post-Stalin era or many South American states, such as Chile and Argentina until relatively recently. However, I do not know and I am unsure that anyone else does either. However, if we are really interested in security in my broader sense, these are issues which it is necessary to examine.

The issue of violence is rather embarrassing for the student of strategy, though not much less embarrassing for the rest of us in this general area. I interpret traditional strategic thought in the contemporary scene as holding that violence is a cost and to be reduced or avoided when practicable. Nevertheless, it is a cost which has to be borne from time to time, and ultimately we are dealing in cost-benefit analysis. The strategist in this mirrors the views of the overwhelming majority of others, at least in Western societies, and most others besides. However, there is a fundamental weakness in this view. Violence is something about which we have deeply ambivalent attitudes. We are partly appalled by it but partly also attracted to it. Warfare, in particular, has always fascinated people, mainly, but by no means exclusively, men and has never lacked people to come along and take part in it. In the case of goals like power and money, those who pursue them are clear about them and, for the most part, are not ambivalent. In the case of violence it is more complex but nevertheless profound, and part of the deep, underlying nature of our make-up. It would be impossible to look at, say, *The Sun* in the Gulf conflict of 1991 or even more in the Falklands War of 1982 and argue that violence was a cost sadly expended. With its usual skill at touching deeply-held impulses, *The Sun* was expressing what a lot of people felt and, though perhaps less crudely expressed, what a lot of people felt who might not quite like *The Sun's* way of putting things. I do not think that anyone in our field has yet really come to terms with this issue. For rather different reasons it is put on one side by all schools of thought, none of which really wants to consider its very damaging implications. I am afraid, however, that it will not go away.

While the conventional strategist is ready to accept the lust for power as a major motive of humans, the underlying premises held by many students of peace studies are basically that human beings are good, though in some cases an exception is made for capitalists. People may pursue power now but, if we get the right conditions, this will cease and violence will solve itself. Like the strategists, they are apt to turn away from the darker forces which attract us to violence. I personally think that people are malleable, though I have a rather bleak view of what is available to be manipulated.

The approaches, therefore, divide as follows. For peace researchers, human beings are fundamentally good and damaged by institutions. In this these researchers follow Rousseau or, more recently, Carl Rogers. Such institutions range from the state, to the family, to the capitalist system, and there are differences in emphasis. However, we should correct the institutions and all will be well. For strategists, human beings are fundamentally combative and probably wicked, and the institutions necessary to contain them are ones involving balances and equilibria so that these impulses may be held in check or, from an optimistic viewpoint, directed in creative directions. In my view, which is a mixed one, the impulses are not all virtuous as the peace researcher often claims, but are mixed with impulses to violence and destruction just as powerful as those to creativity and co-operation. Human beings are malleable in the sense that, in appropriate social structures, they are able to develop the more positive aspects of their personalities; but the whole business is much more precarious than the optimists hope. This puts me on the peace research end of the presuppositional spectrum but with a pessimistic gloss. I would see a concentration on such things as balance, and so on, as short-term requirements, necessary to preserve some semblance of peace, but which risk avoiding the problems, as balances are themselves always likely to be temporary. The goal is to try to seek those structures where at least the tacit rules of the game are relatively non-violent; that is, we have to see how to do without authoritarian states, and devise social structures, whether state or otherwise, whose rulers are *content* to remain non-expansionary as distinct from being *constrained* to remain non-expansionary.

Though the discussion of presuppositions is important in considering the different approaches to international, violent conflict, it is not the whole of the story. International relations as practised by more traditional scholars, and in particular in this country, involves a further set of contested presuppositions. These differences are found in the 'two cultures' of C.P. Snow. The early development of conflict analysis did not come about in an intellectual vacuum. The 1950s and the 1960s were the days of optimism as far as the social sciences were concerned. Odd though it may sound today, Keynesian economics seemed to have solved some crucial economic problems, and the computer seemed to be on the way to cracking the problems of complexity which had been the bugbear of the social scientist. In particular, many branches of the social sciences, and not just economics, were stating theory rigorously and openly welcoming mathematical forms of argument and relying on statistical testing. It was the heyday of the mathematical social scientists, such as Herbert Simon and Paul Samuelson, and the conflict analysts were merely part of this trend. It was natural that Richardson should have been neglected in the 1930s, but, in the right circles at least, venerated (posthumously) in the 1960s. However, many of these people were clearly in a scientific tradition. Some, such as Rapoport, were trained in mathematics and the sciences. Others, such as Boulding, were economists and, as has often been pointed out, economists more than other social scientists have always suffered severely from physics-envy. This continues; the conflict analysts, if not scientists, normally have some mathematical background and have a profound respect for the scientific tradition and regard themselves as firmly within it. Followers of the classical tradition were clearly arts men (there were not many women in either camp). The divide between conflict analysis and classical international relations was not of political opinion but of intellectual tradition. These traditions still pursue distressingly healthy and separate existences. Snow's views apply today with very little modification from 1962 when he first wrote his essay. For all the good it did, he might as well have saved himself the trouble.

As far as Britain was concerned, the scientific dream was one dreamt by Americans and the sooner they woke up from it the better. Their persistent refusal to do so has also been a constant source of puzzlement to many in this country, as has the ability of this school to drug some English yokels, simple but honest souls such as myself, into following its tenets.

Some Problems for the Future

Security against violence comes then in many forms. There is security at the sub-state level viewed as security from others: we are protected, if we are lucky, by the state against the Mafia, the drug barons and so on. Also, if we are lucky and secure, we are defended against the depredations of the state itself in the form of authoritarian dictators who kill and deprive us of our liberty. We are also kept secure against outside predators, and it is on this sort of security that strategic analysts and the like tend to concentrate.

What then are the problems to be tackled over the next few years by people with our interests, irrespective of the label under which they trade? My firm deals in testable hypotheses, or so I would like to hope. We advertise the possibilities of a change in life-style, though only with difficulty. The life-style, though, consists in looking within the state as much as externally. First, let us admit that the security problem of the next decades, if not necessarily the next decade, looks rather bleak. From time to time regimes arise which are violently expansionary and destructive both internally and externally. There is absolutely no reason whatever to suppose that the regime of Saddam Hussein is the last of these. I have no idea where the next such regime will arise but there is little doubt that one will, somewhere and at some time. Further, the enormous damage done by the Iraqi regime was largely in its own general area – though the bill for the ecological damage is still unclear. The Saddam of 20 or 30 years' time may well have rockets which could threaten London, Moscow, New York or Tokyo, and nuclear, chemical or biological warheads to go with them. If 30 years is too short for this scenario then make it 50 or even 100 years, but it will happen as long as the present general political structures continue. There appears to be an assumption that wars can be fought by the powerful Western powers without any essential threat to the homelands, an assumption which seems to be tacitly accepted in popular writing. This seems to me to be false. It cannot go on for ever. The days of the cold war begin to look rather cosy.

What then is to be done? In the short run the answers lie partly with the strategists. The states as they exist at the moment will continue to do so in the near future. What then are stable distributions of power? I do not think this can be presented as a purely technical problem yet, but I hope that we shall move on to that point. Put differently, I do not see why it should not be posed and answered as a technical problem, and furthermore it should be posed and answered as quickly as possible. There are other issues surrounding it. A lot of money is to be made by selling armaments to all and sundry without enquiring too deeply into the desirability of the regime to whom they go, nor into the niceties of regional balances and the like. We have only to look at the armaments honey-pots in the Middle East and the eagerness of many to get their fingers into them to appreciate this point. However, there is no reason to assume that ability to pay has anything whatever to do with creating stability. The notion that market forces are in any way relevant to the distribution of arms is farcical and would never have been entertained for a moment were it not such a convenient doctrine. A major lesson of the conflicts of recent years is that the arms trade should be severely controlled, that arms should be sold with the preservation of stability as the dominant criterion, and that we tackle the issue of the free-rider arms salesman as an issue of urgency. In view of the lack of concern by political leaders on this issue, and the eagerness with which they greet the honey-pot, I have practically no faith whatsoever that this issue will be tackled. It probably never will be until a major First World country is severely threatened by violence; it appears that Israel is not sufficient.

In the longer term we need to know more about what makes states become authoritarian and expansionary. If the world continues as it is then the scenario sketched above is almost inevitable. I have no answers but I suggest some procedures. We must investigate the problem scientifically and formulate hypotheses carefully and in a disciplined manner. We must test carefully and be fully conscious of the grounds for our belief in the propositions we come up with. This is not to say that we have to require certainty before we can act, which is clearly impossible, but we must be aware of the degree of uncertainty we act under. Above all, we must beware of 'conventional wisdom' – it does not seem to work very well. These questions are unanswered as yet.

Finally the issue I raised above of the ambivalent attitudes we all have towards violence must be investigated more closely. Violence is not just an instrumental tool used between states for the pursuit of their goals. This involves both a careful examination of the use of violence in human affairs, but also the recognition of its role in our own thinking. What, indeed, are the motivations which have created our ambiguous attitudes and lead us now to be so concerned with the trade of violence? Conflict analysts have barely considered this question as yet – partly, I suspect, because they have been frightened away by Popper from any serious consideration of any but simplistic motivations in the generally empiricist mode of analysis dominant in the field. I think, however, that these crucial questions can be answered only if we face issues of unconscious motivation squarely, or think it is only something that nasty people like Saddam Hussein suffer from.

I have one final point: security studies, whether under the aegis of international relations, strategy, peace research or conflict research are conducted, for the most part, by secure people in secure societies. Our worries about food are about whether the avocados at Sainsbury's will be ripe this week – not hunger: our contact with violence is with the inconvenience if Charing Cross Station is closed, and does not involve a serious fear of death, though Israeli strategists are in a more precarious position. This gives us a particular perspective and, in general, it is an abstract theoretical topic so far as we are concerned. In order that the really dominant questions of security should be addressed, we have to have the imagination to put ourselves in the position of people who, in fact, live in conditions of fear.

10

Mindless Eclecticism or Creative Synthesis?

Lawrence Freedman

Let me begin with an identity crisis. I have been connected during my working life with university departments of government, political science, social studies and now war studies, and with institutes of strategic studies, international affairs and now defence studies. Furthermore, I could easily have ended up in departments of international relations or arms control or military studies or even peace studies. At one point I would have described myself as a political scientist, but have been happy to be described by others as a diplomatic historian.

None of this labelling has unduly affected my academic interests which have remained reasonably constant throughout. But the confusion of labels must excite suspicion as to whether it implies a confused intellectual identity.

One explanation might be that this identity is not so much confused as sinister, and that the many names represent a search for an inoffensive cover for a perverted fascination with the ways and means of death and destruction – the study that dare not speak its name. On this basis, parading at King's College London under the banner of 'war studies' is the equivalent of coming out, taking pride in a minority taste. However, while I like the name for its rejection of euphemism, it still does not describe an academic discipline. Rather it is a shared subject matter which can be approached, as it is in the Department of War Studies, in an inter-disciplinary manner with contributions from History, Philosophy, Politics, Sociology and Economics.

The field of war studies is also far greater than any individual's capacity. I often seem fated to meet people deeply interested in war studies who seek my opinion on their private thoughts concerning the innately aggressive nature of humankind or the relative merits of different types of gun barrel or the wisdom of Monty's tactics on the second day of El Alamein. As I have no informed view on any of these topics, in each case my interlocutor is left wondering how on

118

earth I got a job teaching a subject about which I am so patently ignorant.

Even in those areas notionally in my expertise, my views do not seem to enjoy any special status as a result. When the great nuclear debate was under way a decade ago all sorts of professional groups from physicians to musicians seemed to feel that they should issue collective statements on the dangers of the arms race. I sometimes wondered about starting 'nuclear strategists for the NHS' or 'the defence specialists linguistic study group'. Of course there is no room for complaint in that the issues at stake in this debate are properly the concern of all citizens rather than of just a specialist group. The experience, however, did leave a lingering question as to where an academic competence ends and mere opinion begins.

Within this broad and confused field of war studies I prefer to call myself a strategist because much of my teaching is of something I call strategic theory and much of my writing is concerned with the development and implementation of military strategies. If this label is to solve my identity crisis I need to be able to demonstrate that it represents a distinctive type of intellectual activity. I set myself the task of demonstrating that Strategic Studies carries with it the potential for synthesising insights drawn from a range of disciplines while at the same time acknowledging that this carries an equal risk of descending into a mindless eclecticism. Whether the strategist succeeds with creative synthesis or fails with mindless eclecticism can at least be judged by a supremely practical test.

Strategy and Marxism

The title of this essay comes from a remark I recall from a seminar at the University of York in the early 1970s. The setting was a rather arcane debate over the theory and method of Political Science. A decade earlier, at the start of the 1960s, the 'behavioralist revolution' had been at its peak in the discipline, encouraging the view that a rigorous empiricism might raise its status to that of a true Science.

By the end of the 1960s this approach was under severe challenge. Critics claimed that Political Science was becoming a discipline which, in failing to achieve such a status, avoided that dangerous subject politics. In the search for phenomena that were in some way measurable, the empiricists were only touching the surface of political life and ignoring the deeper structures of power. In the pretence that being empirical was in some sense value-free they were ignoring the truly controversial and difficult questions at the heart of political debate.

The argument for a much more radical and explicitly normative approach was inspired by the protests over civil rights and Vietnam. It was reinforced by the epistemological naivety with which it is so easy to charge the crude empiricist. In building up this epistemological case a critical text was Thomas Kuhn's *Structure of Scientific Revolutions*. Kuhn demonstrated that natural science had not progressed through the accumulation of verified 'laws'. Rather, at each historical stage, 'normal' science was shaped by a dominant paradigm which was reinforced by the scientific establishment until anomalies began to appear in observed phenomena which could not be explained within the terms of this paradigm and could be encompassed much better by an alternative one. A struggle would then ensue until the old establishment was obliged to give way to the new.

Kuhn's work has generated a large literature among historians of science. My concern now is only to note its influence on political theory. If it was the case that natural science at any time was going to contain a fair share of what would later be exposed as myth, then the empiricists in the social sciences had clearly chosen a wholly illusory model. Some critic went further and suggested that if the struggle to define normal science at any given time was one between competing paradigms then this could be the case in political theory.

Hence the term 'paradigm' was embraced to refer to a conceptual framework which shaped the way political phenomena were both perceived and interpreted. To the extent that we can recognise distinct schools of thought then we might usefully call these paradigms and even watch something equivalent to one of Kuhn's scientific revolutions under way. However, the transfer of Kuhn's theory to political science was in its own way as misleading as had been the attempt by the crude empiricists to ape the traditional view of natural science. For while Kuhn had shown that what passed for normal science at any time was the result of a political struggle within the scientific establishment, it was still the case that the old paradigm became vulnerable through an essentially empirical failure – the theory could not explain evidence that it was becoming increasingly difficult to ignore.

Paradigms often came to be used by political scientists to refer to competing traditions that could never be reconciled because they were based on contrasting philosophical premises – idealism or materialism – and opposed value systems – conservatism or socialism. This approach was particularly favoured by radicals, for its implication was that all political analysis was, in essence, ideological. If every substantive statement only gained meaning through its paradigmatic context then it was not altogether clear what role would be played by evidence and reason in the analysis as well as the conduct of political life.

This then was the background to the question of eclecticism or synthesis. The Marxists in our seminar were arguing that an attempt to borrow from a variety of competing paradigms must be mindlessly eclectic because in their underlying premises they were fundamentally incompatible.

There seemed to me to be two reasons to recoil from this remorseless-polarisation. First, once one gets into the position that everything is determined by structures of thought and language then it is not hard to get into a black hole in which true dialogue and communication are rendered impossible, for every statement – including this one – can be disregarded as inherently ideological. Every concept becomes essentially contested. There is a formidable case to be made for this view in the philosophy of the social sciences, but if taken to its logical conclusion it leads to an analytical dead-end.

My second problem was that the attempt at intellectual polarisation was politically as much as philosophically driven. The soft liberal's waffling, inconclusive, fence-straddling eclecticism infuriates the radical who sees things in terms of stark choices. If the choice really is 'idealism or materialism', 'socialism or barbarism' or 'red or dead' then a refusal to make the choice becomes unconscionable. Sometimes the choice is stark and the middle ground turns out to be a void. However, it seemed to me that the manner in which the choice was framed might be influenced as much by the day's political agenda as by a natural philosophical divide.

Even within Marxism there were clearly a number of distinct currents co-existing uneasily. Intellectually there had been attempts at synthesis with such diverse movements as psychoanalysis and structuralism. Politically the label had been appropriated by groups with diverse constituencies and quite opposed programmes. Moreover, while I found a radical analysis appealing, looking at root causes rather than symptoms and considering the conditionality of the structures within which 'normal' apolitical life is conducted, it did not seem to me that a radical analysis inevitably led to a radical political practice. It could illuminate the hopelessness of such practice as much as its potential. The mixed political record of Marxists underscored this point. Political practice – unlike intellectual debate – necessitated compromises and fudges.

This basic problem with Marxism, which has become far more acute in recent years than it appeared 20 years ago, is relevant because this is the most strategically-conscious of all political traditions. Many working within it have stressed the parallels between the strategic judgements of a general leading his troops into battle and those of a vanguard political party leading the working class to an awareness of its strength. Lenin was as influenced by Clausewitz as any other twentieth century leader. Marxism has claimed not only to be able to understand the workings of society but to have identified the agencies of change within it, and, through this understanding, to be able to guide these agencies to an earlier and more supreme success than would otherwise have been possible.

In the attempt to link theory to practice Marxists, especially those of a Bolshevik inclination, have paid close attention to the strategic possibilities of all political activities from candidature in elections to general strikes, to armed insurrection. This has led to a model strategic debate on the relationship between ends and means – does the moderation in slogans necessary to win elections restrict the scope for the eventual implementation of a full-blooded socialist programme? Does dependence on the strike weapon encourage a limiting focus on industrial power rather than broader political power? Do the inflammatory slogans necessary to stoke the fires of revolution result in an extremist and intolerant regime? Anyone with experience of Marxist politics will be aware of the intensity with which these questions can be debated by groups with no chance whatsoever of discovering the validity or otherwise of their prescriptions. Meanwhile those social democratic political parties that originated out of similar and often more substantial debates of decades ago have now moved on to an appreciation of the realities of power to a point where reminders of their philosophical origins have become something of an embarrassment.

This digression into Marxism suggests three points of wider relevance to the study of strategy. First, the sort of sharp distinctions that serve in a seminar to clarify issues and sharpen differences can become intellectually constricting. Theorists of international relations, for example, too often get stuck with the debate over realism. This debate originated in an attempt to make sense of traumatic events in the first half of this century and as a reaction to the failed idealism of the 1920s. Just as the international system has moved on from that period so must the analysis. Yet it often seems to be the case that strategic studies is identified – by both practitioners and critics – as the last redoubt of an old-fashioned realism. Because it can be shown to be philosophically rooted in realism it must therefore by necessity still base everything on the inherent insecurity of unitary states in an anarchic international system. I would argue that progress in both the theory and the practice of strategy depends on a continuing effort to improve the general understanding of the workings of the international system in all its complexity.

My second point follows from this and also from my earlier observation that the strategic practice of those seeking political power for radical purposes came to involve a synthesis of their programme with elements from others in order to build up the widest possible constituency. Objectives often had to be moderated in order to render them achievable. To the purist this synthesis appears as eclecticism because it requires him to lose sight of and interest in the original purposes, while the compromiser at least can claim something to show for the effort. The same tendencies may be seen in any strategic activity, including that of states in conflict with one another. This dialectic between ends and means, which seems to me to be at the heart of much strategy, strains loyalty to any rigid conceptual or political framework.

This leads on to the third point which concerns the relationship between the theorist and the practitioner. Marx urged that the two should merge into one: the philosophers having hitherto only interpreted society must now change it. A strategically-minded intellectual tradition encourages activism. While, at least in the West, the intellectual origins of strategic studies are quite distinct from Marxism, this activist aspiration is shared.

Strategy and Activism

Such activism would not be expected from a historian, linguist or chemist. However, here strategists are not wholly unique. A comparison may be made with economists who continually address questions of public policy and also often define their distinctive schools – Keynsian, monetarist and indeed Marxist – in terms of their preferred mode of economic management. Many naturally assume that an important part of their task is to service policy-makers.

The economists' model is clearly one that many strategists would like to emulate. This raises a number of issues. It is by no means axiomatic that academic students of strategy make good practical strategists – although in today's university system they get plenty of opportunities to try their hand. Strategic practice, as opposed to the theory, demands risk-taking on behalf of a wider constituency. It involves the mobilising of human and material resources according to a developed plan against anticipated opposition and in pursuit of stated objectives. If the objectives are misplaced, the plan misconceived, the resources unavailable or poorly mobilised, then the strategy will fail and this will be the strategist's responsibility. But an academic strategist advocating a war is not answerable to the families of casualties, and one urging an increase in defence expenditure does not have to find the extra revenue (just as, one might add, an economist advocating a deflationary policy is not answerable to the unemployed).

Despite the obvious analytical advantages that detachment can bring, this lack of accountability ought to trouble academic advisers when they take prominent positions on controversial issues. Those who based their advice on expectations that turned out to be over-gloomy during the Gulf War of 1990–91 may feel their reputations dented, but they can always claim that they were not in full possession of all the latest intelligence. In this case, of course, their advice should have been qualified in the first place. At the very least, academic pundits need to be clear as to whether they are advising on how to achieve the government's objectives or their own.

If the academic is promoting a dissident political programme then the advice may be irrelevant. On the other hand if the academic's analysis becomes tailored to the prejudices of the political establishment then it just becomes part of the conventional wisdom. Indeed, excessive attention to establishment concerns may be intellectually corrupting both in terms of the advisers' natural search for patrons to ensure that their views are given the prominence that they think they deserve, and the narrowness of vision that this must entail.

The strategic practitioner has a responsibility that the academic adviser cannot have. But while responsibility may concentrate the mind it does not inform it. A general entering into battle will base his strategy on a composite set of judgements concerning politics (how best to define the goal of the campaign, the importance of keeping allies sweet, what the people back home will stand), sociology (the likely cohesion of the enemy force under stress), psychology (how to motivate his own men, getting into the mind of the enemy commander), geography (the possible impact of terrain on particular tactics), history (what other generals got away with in similar circumstances), economics (the rate at which he dare expend *matériel* on specific targets), and so on.

Many successful politicians and generals work on intuition and hunch, or draw lessons from experience or remembered bits of history in a manner which would strike an academic as being wholly inappropriate or based on disgracefully exaggerated generalisations. But whether a proper academic methodology would do any better is a moot point, as there is no time for long projects and there can be little tolerance of lots of caveats. When a general is wondering whether an enemy formation might break in the face of a sudden attack, he is not going to be impressed if told that more research is needed or that his working hypothesis is inherently untestable.

Furthermore, the general is not working in isolation. In the Gulf War, for example, the commander of the coalition forces, General Norman Schwarzkopf, in formulating his strategy had to take account of the views of his political masters, including what was at stake for the US President and the constitutional prerogatives of Congress. The views of the senior officers working under him would be important for what they told him not only about the morale, readiness and capabilities of individual units but also the desire of their particular branch of the armed forces for an appropriate share of the action. As part of a coalition of states he would need to be aware of the sensitivities of both Arab and European governments. All this was necessary before he could properly address the vulnerabilities of Iraq.

Thus in developing his strategy to deal with Iraq he needed a strategy to deal with his own side. His optimum course of action would be one which satisfied to the greatest possible extent the many interested parties on whose behalf he was acting. This was far more than merely ensuring that everyone got his quota of the glory. It included such critical matters as the implications of various political considerations, including ultimate objectives, for the conduct of the war.

So while strategic activity is often presented in terms of a conflict between two opposing parties, in practice it involves working within a complicated set of political relationships. The successful strategist must therefore be a master of the creative synthesis, in terms of extracting from the various prescriptions something that will actually work, and will fail if the pressures generate a mindless eclecticism in which the several aspects of the plan fail to relate to each other. This act of synthesis is political and not simply analytical. At stake is not the elegance of the theory but the coherence of the group.

Let me sum up this part of my argument. The strategist's skill depends on relating means to ends. The academic strategist has no special competence when it comes to choosing objectives for a government, but he can at least explain how the choice of objectives might impinge on the course and duration of a conflict. However, such advice must come at something of a discount because the academic is essentially irresponsible. The academic does not actually have to take the fateful decisions which flow from his strategic judgements and is therefore not directly answerable for their consequences. In addition, he does not have to master the decision-making process in order to secure the adoption of a preferred strategy in the light of the pressures emanating from allies, partners and followers as well as enemies.

Strategy After Communism

Nonetheless, public debate on national strategy now assumes an academic input. This input is most effective when it takes one of two quite different forms. The first is to provide a rare expertise that can illuminate aspects of the strategist's problem that would otherwise remain dim; the second is to help to shape the broad understandings of the utility of armed force when dealing with international conflict which can exercise a significant influence on practical strategic debate.

Looking back to the 'golden age' of strategic studies of 30 years ago it is hard not to be struck by the fact that its most original contributions came not just through the application of methodologies which were much more sophisticated than anything else in operation at the time, but because they represented a conceptual breakthrough which has had a lasting effect on the way that we think about strategic issues.

The key insight was to recognise that both East and West could gain if they modified their behaviour to stress certain co-operative goals, of which the most critical was the avoidance of nuclear war, even while recognising that their basic antagonism was deep-rooted and enduring. A sense of the interrelatedness of human behaviour, which must be at the heart of any strategic thinking, encouraged analysis from the perspective of the system as a whole, rather than from that of an individual actor within the system. To an actor tempted to participate in an arms race, it could be suggested that any gains could well be transitory, while, from the broader perspective, any damage to the international system as a whole must eventually damage the actor himself. The goal became less the pursuit of advantage within the system than the stability of the system, leading to proposals for a strategic posture that prevented the adversary from being able to mount effective threats yet avoiding threats to the adversary in return.

The policy conclusions to emerge from all of this were model-driven, but that did not seem to matter because they emerged at a time when the real world situation appeared to conform to the model. Only two superpowers and their allies were involved. The geopolitics of their confrontation reached a natural stand-off in the centre of Europe while its military character was determined by a nuclear stalemate.

Almost three decades of thinking along these lines has left its mark. Stability is now deemed to be the greatest political value so that the role of strategy is to devise methods of securing and sustaining it. However, its pursuit has now become something of a fetish.

It was one thing to give it the highest value when instability was generally considered to be tantamount to the outbreak of a nuclear war. Now instability has lesser connotations how does it compare in our hierarchy of values to the perpetuation of inequality and injustice, or the failure to resolve conflicts that were left in an uneasy truce during the cold war years?

Moreover, the strategic model of stability placed far too much emphasis on the military relationship that was presumed to be found at its core. The safe functioning of the international system was seen to be virtually dependent on the maintenance of a superpower military equilibrium at its centre, working as a sort of gyroscope. Should it spin out of control then tragedy would follow. As we now come out of the cold war we can see that the former political stability shaped, as much as was shaped by, military stability. The association of strategy with nuclear policy and of political stability with mutual assured destruction was misleading.

The unique nature of the nuclear balance reinforced a genuine political balance. Since the late 1980s, the old theory has become largely irrelevant as we come to address a much more politically dynamic situation in which there are far too many variables to make possible a simple model and in which nuclear weapons, at least for the moment, are playing a marginal role.

In current circumstances stability may prove to be a chimera and its pursuit for its own sake futile. The new situation is not one of universal disorder, just as there were obvious limits to the orderly nature of the former situation. The idea we have to give up is that of systemic stability, because the international system is no longer dominated by the superpowers' balancing act. It can no longer be characterised in terms of a simple organising principle. Previous characterisations were based on the underlying relations between the great powers. The alternative to bipolarity was seen as multipolarity and is now seen as unipolarity or combinations in different spheres of activity – multipolarity in the economic, unipolarity in the military. However, at a time when the major powers are able to work together in a relatively co-operative manner, lesser powers are in turmoil. That is, in this post-colonial, as well as post cold-war period, great power relations do not set the terms for the rest of the system.

Many of the interesting strategic questions will reflect on the interaction between the orderly and the disorderly parts of the world. Can the European Community, for example, reach out into the states of the old Soviet empire and help them to mature both politically and economically, or will they lapse back into a narrow and destructive nationalism? Can the major powers, working together through the United Nations Security Council, devise and enforce rules of conduct for international behaviour to prevent conflicts among lesser powers from getting out of hand?

Strategy and Power

If strategic studies is going to be able to contribute to this new situation it needs to reappraise some of its core assumptions. Its conceptual framework must be shown not only to be able to cope with the coming decade but also have something to say retrospectively about what went before. At this point I want to rehearse briefly an argument which I have developed at length elsewhere, which is that strategy must be defined in terms of power.[2] In doing this I intend to integrate some of the strands developed in this essay thus far.

The starting point is a dissatisfaction with the standard definitions of strategy which I have used and encouraged as much as anyone else. For example let us take Liddell Hart's definition of strategy as the distribution and employment of military means to fulfil the ends of policy. This is fine in every respect save that it takes the ends of policy as given, while I have suggested that ends must be geared to what is feasible. Utopianism – or more mildly, idealism – may be defined as a breakdown in strategic thinking in which the gap between what is desired and what can be attained through available means has become hopelessly large. On the other hand, a great strategist might be one capable of bridging what would have seemed to others to be an unbridgeable gap. Strategy seems to me in this sense to be the essence of the politician's art. Parenthetically I would note that while this art is often defined as being 'of the possible', it is only truly an art when it is 'of the improbable'.

My definition of strategy is the art of creating power. Power is generally defined as a capacity to produce effects. It is unusual for any exercise of power to produce the total effect desired. Moreover, the exercise of power may not be that deliberate but it still must be judged in terms of the interests of those both exercising and being exercised by this power. This suggests a measured definition of power as the capacity to produce effects that are more advantageous than would otherwise have been the case.

A can oblige *B* to modify his behaviour through a successful application of force, or through coercive threats (and also inducements), or best of all, because *B* does his bidding without question because he accepts *A's* authority. With all but the direct application of force, the successful exercise of power depends on *B's* understanding of his relationship with *A*.

If by looking at *A's* great strength *B* acts cautiously, then *A* has exerted power. So power is a capacity that exists to the extent that it is recognised by others. The perceptual basis of power should come as no surprise to those who have followed the twists and turns of deterrence theory. Force provides the most extreme expression of power, for that is when its recognition becomes inescapable. Authority is the best form of power because that is when people do what you want through awe or respect.

One feature of this is that the perception of *B* may bear scant resemblance to the intention of *A*. This is a problem with identifying power with the achievement of *will*, for many of the effects involved are unintended or partial. There is a further problem in that the exercise of power is rarely in one direction. Other wilful beings are involved. It is rare in any social system for an actor to be able to disregard pressure of some sort from all the other actors, for this would involve a complete monopoly of power. There is a fundamental difference between exerting 'power over' nature or physical objects, and over other individuals or groups who may have countervailing capabilities of their own.

In most social systems individual actors participate in a multiplicity of political relationships. *B* does not simply need to modify his behaviour because of *A* but also because of *C* and *D* as well. Most decisions are complex and involve a variety of considerations involving other actors. The more dense and complex the social structure, the more difficult the exertion of power, because *B* cannot attend only to the pressures from *A*, unless *C* and *D* share an interest in opposing *A*. This is the point I am seeking to make when pointing to the need of the successful strategist to accommodate the varying interests and prescriptions of those notionally on his 'side'.

Direct coercion is not the only way of encouraging others to act as you would wish. There is a continuum from force to authority in the exercise of power. Of these two, authority is for the more preferable because it is easier to renew than direct force. This is important because any exercise of power is inherently unstable.

Let us examine this last point more fully. The ideal type towards which most discussions of power tend is of *A* wholly controlling *B*'s fate. Absolute control requires a continual application of force. It needs continual renewal. While for hard cases this may be found when necessary, in practice a more relaxed relationship will often be sought, reducing the coercive aspects of the relationship in an effort to develop durable structures which soften the impact of conflict. Conflict will develop within a political community to the extent that institutional forms leave one group feeling disadvantaged, and to the extent that it sees itself to be a distinct community on its own.

The greater the coherence within a political community the more likely it is that power will be exercised through authority. In modern, complex structures this will mean that it has been institutionalised. For reasons that are familiar this is extremely difficult in international society, but it has been achieved in some areas – for example western Europe and North America. Here the complexity of social interactions ensures a coherence that in itself deters secessionists and insurrectionists.

However, this is by no means always the case. Many modern states are still at an early stage of development and are not based on any natural social cohesion. They are agglomerations of nationalities or tribes who feel their greatest loyalty to the group rather than to society at large. This is the problem of the interaction between social structures that vary considerably in their development. Western Europe is a strong sub-system, in that it is marked by a complex interdependence and shared values while eastern Europe is much weaker.

Strategy only comes into being when there is a conflict of which all participants are aware. It is interesting to consider unconscious power relationships but they do not involve strategy. The institutionalisation of advantage so that it becomes reflected in consensus and procedure is the supreme achievement of strategy. Strategists specialise in situations in which force may be necessary, but a sole preoccupation with force misses the opportunities of authority. Although all power is unstable, that based on authority is more durable than that based on force.

Because in most cases, the power relationship between A and B is only one of a number in which both actors participate, B may have a variety of options as to how to respond to A's threats. In order to get B to produce the required behaviour A must gain B's attention and shape his construction of reality. This is always the case even in war. In the movement towards the decisive clash, B may be holding out all the time for a better peace settlement than unconditional surrender. Force may for a moment provide complete control, but the instability of such control requires that either it is renewed continuously or else transformed, through the strategist's art, into authority.

While military strategists naturally think in terms of direct force this is only part of a continuum and as an option it must be judged against other means of creating power. Political leaders, whose everyday experience of power revolves around well-institutionalised authority may find it difficult to grasp the approach of opponents from different regions and cultures for whom the experience is more of a crude struggle for survival.

If, as I have suggested, tensions between the more and the less stable parts of the world are likely to characterise future international politics then – as we saw in the Gulf War – this divergent experience of power can be significant.

Within the industrialised world political stability is the product of social and economic complexity and institutionalised power structures based on recognised authority. All this helps to marginalise the importance of armed force. Force becomes important only when challenges to these structures arise. The role of force in European affairs is likely to result from the breakdown of established structures in the old Communist bloc where legitimacy has been drained from anyone associated with the old regimes.

In thinking about the future use of armed force by the West we need to focus on a quite different set of problems to the former preoccupation with military balance. There are, of course, lingering aspects of this concern so long as Russia or other states of the former Soviet Union retain some of the attributes of a superpower. However, Western security is no longer so much at risk from an opposing Eastern bloc of comparable strength as from the disruptive consequences of breakdown in the east. The role of armed force, as compared with other forms of power in all of this, remains uncertain: obviously the current interest is in economic reconstruction, legitimate political institutions and accepted rules for international behaviour. However, as news from the Balkans reminds us, this may be easier said than done.

What then does all this mean in terms of the original concern with the status of strategic studies? In arguing that strategy is the art of creating power I have tried to link the study to its core focus. Of course, the study of politics in general is often defined as the study of power. Strategic studies is different not only because it is more interested in force than in other forms of power, but because it addresses power from the perspective of those wielding it.

It has been a natural preoccupation of political theory to seek to tame power, to render it accountable and its operations predictable. The benefits of an ordered society with low levels of violence are self-evident. But in the process our understanding of agencies of change may have been undermined, a loss reinforced by the fact that those most preoccupied with this question have come from the left and have – by and large – got it wrong.

The same tendency is apparent in international theory which has sought to transfer these benefits of order to the world as a whole, and strategic studies has been seen either as an opponent or as an accomplice in this effort, according to which particular branch of international relations theory is adopted. Yet by focusing on the actors within the system and their sense of their own interests and aspirations, strategic studies must be subversive. It encourages the analysis of those situations where order is absent or else where disorder is encouraged by those who believe that it will be to the advantage of those on whose behalf they are acting.

By definition, the exercise of power in conditions of relative stability is somewhat easier than in conditions of relative instability, when there are far more variables in play and their interaction is quite uncertain. This condition is the most demanding for the strategist, but – again almost by definition – it is not one likely to support a unified theory. In this sense strategy may be unavoidably eclectic. Whether the eclecticism is creative or mindless in the end is up to the strategist's art.

References and Notes

Introduction

1. An excellent discussion of these points is to be found in Joseph S. Nye, *Bound to Lead: the changing Nature of American Power*, New York: Basic Books, 1991.

Chapter 1: Strategic Thinking in Diplomacy: A Legacy of the ColdWar

1. Interview with Hella Pick, *The Guardian*, 26 February 1990.
2. 'US Actions toward China', Acting Secretary Lawrence S. Eagleburger's statement before the Senate Foreign Relations Committee, 7 February 1990, *Current Policy, No.1247*, US Department of State, Bureau of Public Affairs, Washington, DC, February 1990, p.1.
3. Ibid, p.2.
4. Ibid.
5. Nakasone Yasuhiro, 'Japan's Choice: a Strategy for World Peace and Prosperity', Alastair Buchan Memorial Lecture, London: International Institute for Strategic Studies, 11 June 1984.
6. Paul Gordon Lauren, 'Theories of bargaining with threats of force: deterrence and coercive diplomacy', in: Paul Gordon Lauren, [ed.], *Diplomacy: New Approaches in History, Theory, and Policy*, New York: Free Press, 1979, p.186.
7. For an early discussion of the proliferation of strategic studies in the USA, see Gene M. Lyons & Louis Morton, *Schools for Strategy: Education and Research in National Security Affairs*, New York: Praeger, 1965. A listing of institutes throughout the world is to be found in *Survey of Strategic Studies*, London: Institute for Strategic Studies, Adelphi Paper 64, January 1970.
8. Bradley S. Klein, 'After strategy: the search for a post-modern politics of peace', *Alternatives*, Vol.XIII, No.3, July 1988, p.300.
9. Remarks made by a crisis management specialist in the State Department. Thomas B. Allen, *War Games*, London: Heinemann, 1987, p.250.
10. Harold Nicolson, *The Evolution of Diplomatic Method*, London: Constable, 1954, p.84.
11. Adam Watson, *Diplomacy: the Dialogue between States*, London: Eyre Methuen, 1982, p.11.
12. B.H. Liddell Hart, *Strategy: the Indirect Approach*, London: Faber, 1967, p.325.
13. Central Policy Review Staff, *Review of Overseas Representation*, London: HMSO, 1977, pp.x–xi, para.8. This document, commonly known as the *Berrill*

Report, had the examination of British overseas representation as its remit, but devoted its introduction to a consideration of the basic objectives of British foreign policy.

14. Ref. 11.
15. Gordon A. Craig & Alexander L. George, *Force and Statecraft: Diplomatic Problems of Our Time*, Oxford: Oxford University Press, 1983, p.12.
16. Ibid.
17. Quoted from an early treatise on ambassadorial functions by Ermalao Barbaro Ibid.
18. Ibid. See also François de Callières, *De la Manière de Négocier avec les Souverains*, Paris: Michel Brunet, 1716, p.46.
19. De Callières, pp.176–77; ref. 10, pp.62–8.
20. Sun Tzu, *The Art of War* (translated by Samuel B. Griffith), Oxford: Clarendon Press, 1963.
21. Michael Howard, 'The classical strategists', in: *Problems of Modern Strategy: Part I*, London: Institute for Strategic Studies, Adelphi Paper 54, February 1969, p.18.
22. Livingston Merchant, 'New techniques in diplomacy', in: E.A.J. Johnson [ed.], *The Dimensions of Diplomacy*, Baltimore: Johns Hopkins Press, 1964, p.133.
23. Maurice Pearton, *The Knowledgeable State: Diplomacy, War and Technology since 1830*, London: Hutchinson, 1982, p.13.
24. Niccolò Machiavelli, *The Discourses* (ed Bernard Crick), Harmondsworth: Penguin, 1970, p.441.
25. Sheldon S. Wolin, *Politics and Vision: Continuity and Innovation in Western Political Thought*, Boston: Little, Brown, 1960, pp.245, 248, 261–2.
26. He had tried but failed to be appointed Prussian Minister in London. Gordon A. Craig, 'On the nature of diplomatic history: the relevance of some old books,' in ref. 6, pp.31, 41 note 68.
27. Ref. 10, p.50. For a brief explanation of the evolution of the idea of *ius naturale* and its reinforcement of the Roman concept of the *ius gentium*, see J.L. Brierly, *The Law of Nations: an Introduction to the International Law of Peace*, Oxford: Clarendon Press, 1928, pp.9–18.
28. De Callières (ref. 18) pp.54–6, translated in Nicolson (ref. 10), p.63–64. Machiavelli, too, argued against the use of threats on the grounds of prudence. *Discourses* (ref. 24), pp.361–2.
29. Ann Waswo, 'The transformation of rural society, 1900–1950', in: Peter Duus [ed.], *The Cambridge History of Japan, Vol.6: The Twentieth Century*, Cambridge: Cambridge University Press, 1988, p.578.
30. Raymond L. Garthoff, *Soviet Military Policy: A Historical Analysis*, London: Faber, 1966, pp.87, 191.
31. '. . . all but one of the major departures in American policy toward nuclear weapons were initially conceived by scientists: the Baruch Plan, the hydrogen bomb, the development of tactical nuclear weapons, the ballistic missile, and a nuclear test ban. Only the doctrine of massive retaliation originated elsewhere.' Robert Gilpin, *American Scientists and Nuclear Weapons Policy*, Princeton: Princeton University Press, 1962, p.37.
32. The bomb plot was mentioned without any comment in his memoirs (pp.38–9). At Yalta he insisted that even if Hitler and his associates were killed or disappeared and another group of people offered unconditional surrender and

the three powers agreed that they were worth dealing with, 'the terms of surrender which had been worked out would be laid before them;' W.S. Churchill, *The Second World War, Vol.VI: Triumph and Tragedy*, London: Reprint Society, 1956, p.290.

33. W.W. Rostow, 'The planning of foreign policy', in ref. 22, pp.43, 53–4.
34. Some strategists, notably Charles de Gaulle, warn against the dangers of depending on doctrine and neglecting the all-important *'force des circonstances'*. Jean Lacouture, *De Gaulle: I.Le Rebelle 1890–1944*, Paris: Editions du Seuil, 1984. However, de Gaulle's conduct of foreign policy was founded on strategic principles. As summarised by Lacouture: *'Les relations entre Etats – alliés ou non – ne sont fondées que sur la force et la ruse'*, *De Gaulle: II. Le Politique 1944–1959*, Paris: Editions du Seuil, 1985, p.623.
35. Ref. 33, pp.53–4.
36. Henry Kissinger, *The White House Years*, London: Weidenfeld & Nicolson and Michael Joseph, 1979, p.195.
37. Eduard Shevardnadze answering readers' letters in *Pravda*, 26 June 1990, (*The Guardian*, 27 June 1990).
38. Paul Kennedy, *The Rise and Fall of the Great Powers*, London: Unwin Hyman, 1988.
39. Ref. 15, p.205.

Chapter 2: Security in a New Age?

1. Erich Fromm, *The Anatomy of Human Destructiveness*.
2. Thomas Hobbes, *Leviathan*, London: Penguin, 1968, Introduction, p.83.

Chapter 3: Madness under Fire

1. *Daily Telegraph*, 18 December 1990.
2. *The Times Literary Supplement*, 18 January 1991.

Chapter 4: Politics as Government and Politics as Security

1. See, Michael Clarke, 'Comparative and international politics: a strange divide', *Politics*, Vol.6, No.2, 1986.
2. The essence of comparative politics is captured in Aristotle, *The Politics*, Harmondsworth: Penguin Books, 1974. The essence of international politics is encapsulated in Kenneth, Waltz, *Man, the State and War: A Theoretical Analysis*, New York: Columbia University Press, 1954. Twentieth century international politics is still well-expressed in E.H. Carr, *The Twenty Years Crisis: 1919–1939*, New York: Harper & Row, 1964.
3. See Barry Buzan, *People, States and Fear: the National Security Problem in International Relations*, Brighton: Wheatsheaf, 1983.
4. Michael Nicholson, *Formal Theories in International Relations*, Cambridge: Cambridge University Press, 1989.

5. See, for example, Joseph Nye, 'The contribution of strategic studies: future challenges', in: *The Changing Strategic Landscape*, Adelphi Paper 235, London: International Institute for Strategic Studies, 1989; Lawrence Freedman, 'Strategic studies', in: Steve Smith [ed.] *International Relations: British and American Perspectives*, Oxford, Basil Blackwell, 1985; Ken Booth, *Strategy and Ethnocentrism*, London: Croom Helm, 1979.
6. See Robert Keohane & Joseph Nye, *Transnational Relations and World Politics*, Cambridge, MA: Harvard University Press, 1971; and *Power and Interdependence*, Boston: Little, Brown, 1977.

Chapter 5: The Evolution of the Concept of Security in International Relations

1. Count Galeazzo Ciano, *Ciano's Diary 1937–1938*, London: Methuen, 1952, pp.167–72.
2. See, for example, his two classic works, *Peace and War: a Theory of International Politics*, London: Weidenfeld Nicolson, 1966; and *On War: Atomic Weapons and Global Diplomacy*, London: Secker & Warburg, 1958.
3. See G.W.F. Hegel, *The Phenomenology of the Spirit*, Ch.IV, 'Autonomy and dependence of self-consciousness: master and slave'.

Chapter 6: Economics and Security: The Disciplines and The Reality

1. See *International Security*, Vol.12, No.4, Spring 1988, pp.5–27.
2. Susan Strange [ed.], *Paths to International Political Economy*, London: Allen & Unwin, 1984.
3. See Edward Luttwak, 'The materialist bias: why we need more "fraud, waste, and mismanagement" ', in his *The Pentagon and the Art of War*, New York: Simon & Schuster, 1985.

Chapter 7: War and The Nation-State: Retrospect and Prospect

1. See Anthony Giddens, *The Nation-State and Violence*, London: Polity, 1985; Michael Mann, *A History of Power from the Beginning to AD 1760*, Cambridge: Cambridge University Press, 1987; Christopher Dandeker, *Surveillance, Power and Modernity*, London: Polity, 1990.
2. Charles Moskos, 'Armed forces in a warless society', unpublished paper delivered to the British Military Studies Group, Annual Conference, King's College London, 1990; F. Fukuyama, 'The end of History?', *National Interest*, Summer 1989, pp.3–18.
3. Giddens, The Nation-State and Violence, op. cit., p.172.
4. R. Bendix, *Nation-Building and Citizenship*, New York: Doubleday, 1969, pp.128–9.

5. Ibid.
6. C.E. Ashworth & Christopher Dandeker, 'Warfare, social theory and west European development', *Sociological Review*, Vol.35, No.1, February 1987, pp.1–18.
7. James Burk, 'National attachments and the decline of mass armed force', *Journal of Political and Military Sociology*, Vol.17, Spring, 1989, pp.65–81. I have also drawn on an unpublished paper by Burk on the decline of mass armed forces and national variations in this and the next few paragraphs.
8. On these issues see P. Manigart, 'The decline of the mass armed force in Belgium', *Forum*, Vol.9 (Sozialwissenschftliches Institut der Bundeswehr), 1990, pp.37–64.
9. I would like to acknowledge my use of W. Von Bredow's stimulating paper on these issues, delivered at a conference in Marburg in 1990, on which I have drawn for some of these formulations.
10. D. Held 'Farewell the nation-state?, *Marxism Today*, December 1988, pp.12–17.
11. Ibid. p.16.
12. Moskos, op. cit.
13. Ibid. p.1.
14. Martin Edmonds, *Armed Services and Society*, Leicester: Leicester University Press, 1988, pp.120–135.
15. Will Hutton, *The Guardian*, 23 January 1991, p.15.

Chapter 8: International Lawyers and Security in the 1990s

1. In 1991 I organised, in cooperation with the Centre for Defence Studies and with Greenpeace, the London Conference on "A 'Fifth Geneva' Convention on the Protection of the Environment in Time of Armed Conflict?". This brought together leading practitioners and experts and resulted in, Glen Plant, *Environmental Protection and the Law of War*, London: Belhaven Press, 1992. There has been extensive debate of the issue in the UN and ICRC since.

Chapter 9: Security in the 1990s and Beyond

1. J. David Singer, *Resort to Arms: International and Civil Wars, 1816–1980*. Beverley Hills and London: Sage, 1982.
2. L.F. Richardson, *Statistics of Deadly Quarrels*, Pittsburg: Stevens, 1960.
3. Harrison Wagner, 'The theory of games and the balance of power', *World Politics*, Vol.XXXVIII, No.4, pp.546–76.
4. A.K. Sen, *Poverty and Famines: An Essay on Entitlement and Deprivation*, Oxford: Clarendon Press, 1981.
5. Bruce Bueno de Mesquita, *The War Trap*, New Haven: Yale University Press, 1981; Michael Nicholson, 'The conceptual bases of The War Trap', *Journal of Conflict Resolution*, Vol.31 No.2, 1987, pp.346–69.
6. Bertrand Russell, *Power: A New Social Analysis*, London: Allen and Unwin, 1938.

Chapter 10: Mindless Eclecticism or Creative Synthesis?

1. Thomas S. Kuhn, *The Structure of Scientific Revolutions*, Chicago: Chicago University Press, 2nd. edn, 1970.
2. Lawrence Freedman, 'Strategic Studies and the problem of power', in: Lawrence Freedman, Paul Hayes and Robert O'Neill [eds.], *War Strategy and International Politics*, Oxford: Oxford University Press, 1992, pp.279–94.

Index

THREE DAY LOAN
This book is to be returned on
or before the date stamped below

UNIVERSITY OF PLYMOUTH

PLYMOUTH LIBRARY
Tel: (01752) 232323
This book is subject to recall if required by another reader
Books may be renewed by phone
CHARGES WILL BE MADE FOR OVERDUE BOOKS